SHARP:
Simple Strategies to Boost Your Brainpower

Heidi Hanna, PhD

DEDICATION

*This book is dedicated to
the millions of caregivers who unconditionally love and support those
with Alzheimer's disease and other forms of dementia.*

*While we continue to work hard to find a cure,
may we all live a life that enables us to be
as healthy and happy as possible,
right here and now.*

*Bringing not only more years to our life,
but more life to our years.*

CONTENTS

ACKNOWLEDGMENTS

Many people dream of writing a book, but for me...well, I always dreamed of writing an acknowledgments page. Seriously. I would sit up late at night thinking about all the people I wanted to thank for my journey before I had a clue where it would actually lead me. I am overwhelmingly inspired by my family, friends, and the clients I've had the opportunity to get to know along the way. Your stories of perseverance and bravery push me to do whatever it takes to continue this work. I am truly grateful!

First and foremost to my incredible family. Dad, thank you for being my #1 fan and the best coach in the world. You taught me from a very early age to dream big, and believed in me even when I didn't believe in myself. Mom, you're my rock. Thank you for always keeping me grounded and reminding me that I am loved, unconditionally. To my brother, Tony and his wife, Willow, thank you for demonstrating to me what it means to be truly dedicated parents and for bringing me the two most special kids in my life, Brady and Lexi. And to my "bonus mom," Jami, thank you for being brave enough to open the blinds for me from time to time.

To my second family at *SYNERGY*, especially Jacquelyn Mack, thank you for holding me accountable and being so passionate about our shared mission. To my fabulous research assistant, Stephanie Matos, thank you for your hard work and dedication to quality.

To the "pioneers" in my career, Chris Osorio, Dana Klein, and Trevor Lauer, thank you for believing in me and for your continued guidance and encouragement, especially early on. To my amazing mentors, Dr. Jim Loehr and Dr. Jack Groppel, I feel honored to have learned from the best and hope that I continue to make you proud.

To my "sole sisters" and Team In Training teammates Robin Grasso, Andrea Canny, and Colleen Legge, thank you for your support and friendship. To my "counselor on the run," Kristine Entwistle for listening to me go on and on and on during our training runs and races and for always being a fantastic sounding board and friend.

To my friends at Janus, including the sales directors around the US and the globe – and especially the Janus Labs team, including Tracy Thomas and John Evans – thank you for your continued encouragement and support.

To the colleagues I've had the honor and privilege of working with along the way – especially Theresa Robinson, Tara Gidus, Bill McAlpine, George Dom, Admiral Ray Smith, and Ron Woods – thank you for inspiring me with your gifts of excellence in teaching and coaching. Thank you to Randy Glasbergen for helping me to laugh more, and allowing me to use his fabulous comics in this book, and to my amazing editor and writing coach, Adam Martin, for your support and guidance throughout this adventure. Hopefully the first of many!

NOTE TO READER

The information made available through *SYNERGY* and the book *SHARP: Simple Strategies to Boost Your Brainpower* is not intended to replace the services of a physician. Content in this book and on our web site is provided for informational purposes only and is not a substitute for professional medical advice. You should not use the information from this program for diagnosing or treating a medical or health condition. Please consult a physician on all matters relating to your health, particularly with respect to any symptoms that may require diagnosis or medical attention. Before implementing any changes to your nutrition and fitness regimen, talk with your doctor. Obtain medical clearance before beginning an exercise program.

Any action in response to the information provided in this book is at the reader's discretion. The author and publisher have checked with sources believed to be reliable in their efforts to provide information that is complete and generally in accord with the standards accepted at the time of publication. However, in view of the possibility of human error or changes in medical sciences, neither the author nor the publisher nor any other party who has been involved in the preparation or publication of this work warrants that the information contained herein is in every respect accurate or complete, and they are not responsible for any errors or omissions or for the results obtained from the use of such information.

SYNERGY and the book *SHARP: Simple Strategies to Boost Your Brainpower* make no representations or warranties with respect to any information offered or provided on or through the program materials regarding treatment, action, or application of medication, and are not liable for any direct or indirect claim, loss, or damage resulting from use of this book or any web sites linked from it.

INTRODUCTION

Have you ever gotten to the point where you find your computer is acting sluggish? Maybe the software doesn't seem to be cutting it anymore. Connections take longer and interruptions become more frequent. From time to time you might even experience a crash. The system just shuts down for no reason and you have to reboot, hoping that things will return to normal even when you know they probably won't. After the meltdown you lose all of your hard work and swear that you will never make the mistake of not saving your work regularly… until you forget, again. (And, yes, I say this from way too much experience.)

Now, just for a moment, think of your life as that balky computer. Do you feel sluggish and less productive than you used to feel? Do you feel as if it takes longer to do the things you once did with ease? Do you feel more easily distracted? Ever experience an energy crash at the end of the day, knowing you need more sleep than you can possibly get to fully recharge your body and mind? Or maybe you've ended up sick, injured, or burned out, promising that you will never let yourself get to this point again but quickly recognizing you don't have enough hours in the day to make taking care of yourself a priority. The signs are clear: You are in serious need of an upgrade. It's time to create a new operating system for your life, one that works best with this fast-paced, constantly connected, 24/7, on-the-go lifestyle.

Although scientists once believed that our brain was hardwired and could not be modified, recent studies show that the way our mind works is actually quite adaptable, if given the right instructions. Similar to how we train the body, a cognitive fitness training program that uses scientifically validated principles of stress and recovery can improve your ability to take on life's challenges. And there are many challenges. Consider this your user's guide for upgrading your life's operating system – a unique way to improve your performance without compromising your health and happiness.

The human system was designed to survive, and the fact that you are reading this book means that your ancestors were good at doing just that. But in today's world the same processes that are meant to protect us can slow us down and make us weak, compromising our performance, engagement, health, and happiness. Our fight-or-flight response fuels us to be able to fight off threats or run away from danger. But a survival-based operating system interprets every stressor as an emergency, which amps up your nervous system and builds up toxic stress hormones in your body. The human system intuitively fears running out of energy. As a result, it will use any means necessary – often harmful ones – to prevent excess use of precious resources.

In times of famine, our body responds by slowing metabolism, stimulating appetite, and increasing fat stores. Movement is intuitively perceived as a waste of precious energy, which leads us to use shortcuts whenever possible (think escalators, elevators, and drive-thrus). Even though it's quite clear that most of us are not in danger of running out of food anytime soon, our brain can still perceive the ups and downs of modern life as signaling an energy emergency. Going too long without eating, sitting for long periods of time, unbalanced stress, lack of sleep, and feeling isolated are some of the biggest threats in our evolutionary past, yet many of us have started to accept them as just part of a typical day. As a result, we compromise our ability to accomplish the goals that are most important to us.

Fortunately, we don't have to live this way. We have choices, and if we choose to strategically upgrade our operating systems – our body (the hardware) and our mind (the software) – we can go from surviving to thriving. Fast.

This user's guide draws on the proven techniques and time-tested approaches of a physical fitness program, targeting one of the most important parts of the body that often gets left behind in our training efforts – our brain. Different strategies are recommended depending on your current level of cognitive (or mental) fitness; beginner, intermediate, or advanced. In order to create a unique program that's customized to your goals, the first step is completing a cognitive fitness assessment designed to help identify challenges and potential growth opportunities. The assessment will call to your attention which strategies will give you the biggest return on your investment.

You can start here or jump straight to the section that you believe will be most beneficial based on your current circumstances. To keep this program practical, applicable, and most importantly sustainable, we will focus on those concepts that are critical to helping you build and maintain your overall cognitive fitness. My rule here is "simplify it to apply it." As the influential German painter Hans Hofmann once said, "The ability to simplify means to eliminate the unnecessary so that the necessary may speak."

Using the *SHARP* solution, including Simple strategies, Helpful tools, Accountability, Routine, and Practice, helps to remind you of the most important fundamentals needed to make your *SHARP* plan stick. Because there is a wealth of information available to take your program to the next level, additional resources are provided at the end of the book if you wish to pursue this aim.

What is Cognitive Fitness?

When we use the word "fitness" we are usually referring to physical fitness, or the capacity to do work. The most commonly used definition of physical fitness comes from the U.S. Department of Health & Human Services (1996): "A set of attributes that people have or achieve relating to their ability to perform a physical activity." The components of health-related physical fitness are strength, flexibility, and cardiovascular fitness, or endurance. In order to be physically fit, all three need to be developed, and maintained, through training. So what does it take to be *cognitively fit?* Not surprisingly, the components aren't that different.

Why is Cognitive Fitness important? 3 critical results
1. Performance

Everybody is looking for an edge to help them stand out from the competition. With only so much time and energy, how do we make ourselves as *SHARP* as possible so we can perform at our best, be positive and resilient, and stay focused on what is most important to us? Researchers in the fields of neuroscience, psychology, and physiology have demonstrated that brain training exercises can have both immediate and long-term effects when practiced regularly. And this conclusion couldn't come at a better time, as the strain on mental energy is at an all-time high.

Times have changed, and yet our minds continue to run on a fairly old-fashioned system. Our current chaotic environment is filled with distractions, causing us to multitask constantly. Despite being a top request of job interviewers, multitasking is not a skill to be developed but rather a bad habit that needs to be eliminated. Numerous studies have demonstrated that multitasking dumbs us down, quickly taking the IQ of a Harvard grad student and turning it to that of an 8 year-old. Yet, even though the negative impact of multitasking has been well documented and published in multiple media channels, the actual act of re-training the brain to stay focused on one thing at a time takes a serious commitment.

Just knowing that we *should* do something has never been the solution – it takes practice. I love what Rick Hanson says about multitasking in his book *Buddha's Brain*: "Multitasking is the art of distracting yourself from two things you'd rather not be doing by doing them simultaneously."[1] This can be a tempting approach to taking a mental timeout, but not one that is effective or efficient when it comes to the people and things that matter most to us.

One of the main complaints I hear from my clients is the constant sense of "busyness" that they feel throughout the day. This sense of feeling overwhelmed leads to decreased productivity and engagement in the workplace. It's estimated that disengaged employees cost US businesses $300 billion every year due to absenteeism, lower productivity, turnover, errors, and accidents.[2]

2. Resilience

In addition to compromising performance, the increasing demands we experience over time also stimulate a chronic stress pattern that is lethal to the human system. The unmanaged stress of our current work environment causes serious disengagement in people's personal lives. According to the 2008 State of Health in the American Workforce Survey, one-third of employees report that their work has a primarily negative impact on their lives off the job by draining their energy, so they don't have enough left over for their personal or family life.[3] Employees are doing more with less as businesses cut back support staff, increase minimum production levels, reduce compensation structures, and so on.

The toll that stress takes on our body, mind, and spirit has been well documented – as we will discuss in the section on stress management (step 3, rule 3).

3. Longevity

As if busyness and stress weren't enough, we all know that… well… we aren't getting any younger. While we continue to extend our lifespan through advances in science and medicine, diseases that are common in aging are becoming more and more of an epidemic. This year marks a turning point for our large baby boomer population: the first year that this generation starts to turn 65, the approximate age when the risk of developing Alzheimer's disease or other forms of dementia begins to increase rapidly. Reach the age of 85, and your risk of having Alzheimer's disease becomes a coin toss. From 2000 – 2006, major health issues significantly decreased in scope except for one, Alzheimer's disease, which nearly doubled.[4] Unfortunately, the current lifestyle most people live only enhances the deterioration process.

The good news is researchers are discovering that our fate may be more in our own hands than we once thought. Healthy living can boost the number of brain cells we have, the number of connections between cells, the strength of each individual cell and its connections, and the stimulation of brain chemicals that fuel cell growth, or neurogenesis. Unfortunately, not enough people are aware of just how much our day to day choices impact our future.

A fascinating discovery in Alzheimer's research happened as a result of the famous nun study.[5] Upon autopsy, it was found that many of the women who had clearly developed tangles and plaques in their brain actually had shown no symptoms of the disease. Knowing firsthand the impact that Alzheimer's has on daily life, I found this shocking!

But if you consider what's happening in the brain when we exercise, eat right, and include the other healthy habits we will talk about in the *Fab 5*, it makes perfect sense. With more cells, more connections, and stronger connections, there are more options for the brain to communicate and function successfully, despite the plaques and tangles that might otherwise get in the way. Kind of like finding out that a bridge has gone out and we need to find another path, but having plenty of quick options to use as a detour. Considering that I have had three grandparents diagnosed with Alzheimer's, this finding caught my attention (and prompted an email to my family members in hopes of motivating them to pursue healthy habits.).

So we may be able to live longer, but the question is, are we living better? As *Blue Zones* author Dan Buettner states, "It's not just about adding more years to your life, but adding more life to your years."[6] With the right cognitive fitness training program, we can extend our lives and stay healthier longer, allowing us to enjoy our time to the fullest.

Starting with a Healthy Foundation

First and foremost you must create a healthy foundation on which to build a fitness program. A smoker shouldn't expect to get maximum benefits from a cardiovascular training session (although many people still try), and someone training an injured muscle wouldn't expect to have an extraordinary strength training workout. In order for your training to yield maximum benefit, it's essential to first support your system through healthy habits that nurture the growth environment and provide the energy needed to fuel progress. For this reason, we begin our cognitive fitness training program with a discussion of how to promote optimal brain health. The *SYNERGY Fab 5* highlights the most important aspects of a healthy lifestyle that directly impact the health and function of your brain. By utilizing these strategies you create the best possible environment for your brain to benefit from the training routine you implement.

Cognitive Fitness Training

With a healthy foundation established, we create the ideal environment to support the growth process. From here we can begin to train strategically. Considering how the brain works, each element of cognitive functioning can be compared to a dimension of fitness.

We will develop mental muscle through a strength building regimen designed to help strengthen the communication pathways in the brain for more secure connections that are easier and easier to navigate. Our strength training program consists of specific strategies that help build stronger neurons, recruit additional neurons for increased speed and accuracy, and improve our resistance to harmful things like distractions and multitasking.

Similar to flexibility training for the body, improving mental flexibility develops our ability to be resilient and to manage stress more effectively so that it enhances us rather than hinders us. Strategies such as positivity training, initiating the relaxation response, and adapting our mindset help to provide resilience to stress and increase balance in our lives.

Finally, like endurance training for the body, which improves the efficiency of our heart and lungs to keep us going over time, mental endurance training requires a similar approach so that we can maintain longevity, staying healthy throughout the aging process. This type of training incorporates elements of strength and flexibility training, in a "cross training" format for maximum impact, and emphasizes strategies and techniques that maximize sustainability. In order to have peak cognitive fitness, we must include a variety of training approaches that support and build upon each other.

Each training section in Part Three outlines the what, why, and how for exercising that element. For each area I have highlighted those techniques that have been scientifically validated to be most effective up until now, in addition to listing a range of other options with substantial potential. For occasions when you can only afford to spend 2 minutes or less, I have recommended *"SHARP Sprints."* To get the most return on your time and energy investment, I have highlighted strategies that will provide cross training benefits among multiple dimensions of fitness, similar to how yoga has the potential to provide strength, flexibility, and endurance improvements to the body (and brain, as we will soon discuss), all in one exercise session.

Where Do I Begin?

In picking up this book you have already taken the first step toward improving your cognitive fitness – that's your initial commitment. You realize that there is something you could be doing a bit differently, potentially better. You want to strengthen your cognitive abilities and get a greater edge so you can perform better. In order to provide you with the greatest return on your investment, we will start by taking a look at your current level of cognitive fitness to determine your best opportunities for immediate improvement.

Having small wins early in your training program will help provide the confidence and motivation you need to continue on your journey towards better cognitive health and fitness. Let's begin!

Copyright 2001 by Randy Glasbergen.
www.glasbergen.com

"No, I don't think you're crazy. Like most of us,
you're just a victim of bad programming."

PART ONE – BOOST BRAIN HEALTH

STEP ONE
Assess Your Cognitive Health & Fitness

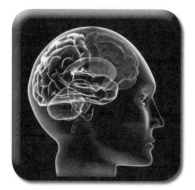

Use this assessment to identify key areas of focus for your own training program. Check any of the following that are true for you, and total the number of checkmarks at the end of each section. This assessment may also be downloaded in a PDF format at www.synergyprograms.com.

#1 Nutrition – Food is Fuel

____ I eat something every 3-4 hours during the day

____ I eat balanced meals and snacks (approximately 25% protein, 25% whole grains, and 50% fruits & veggies at meals, with healthy snacks as needed)

____ I do not drink more than 2 servings of alcohol on any given day (not an average)

____ I very seldom consume portions that are larger than what would make me feel physically satisfied

____ I regularly consume foods with high nutritional value (fruits and vegetables, fish and other lean protein, nuts, seeds and other healthy fats, and whole grains)

____ I eat fatty fish at least 2 times per week or take a fish oil supplement

Total for section #1 = _____

#2 Physical Activity – Activity is Activating

____ I never sit for longer than 90 minutes at one time

____ I get at least 60 minutes of general activity each day

____ I am able to get outside for fresh air/sunshine on a daily basis

____ I get at least 30 minutes of moderate intensity cardiovascular activity a minimum of 3x a week

____ I do full body strength training exercises a minimum of 2x a week

____ I stretch regularly after exercise

Total for section #2 = _____

#3 Stress Management – Balanced Stress is Balanced Life

____ I feel as though I balance my stress levels in a healthy way (not relying on substances like alcohol to calm down)

____ I regularly practice relaxation strategies (meditation, yoga, massage, etc)

____ I very seldom feel frustrated, angry, or irritable

____ I usually feel positive and see challenges as opportunities, rather than pessimistic or in "survival mode"

____ I enjoy challenges at work and do not feel threatened by failure

____ When work is over I am able to turn it off and focus on other things

Total for section #3 = _____

#4 Sleep – Resting is Working
____ I sleep at least 7 hours each night
____ I wake up feeling rested in the morning
____ I do not feel sleepy or lethargic during the day
____ I wake up in the morning when I want, without setting an alarm clock
____ I fall asleep within 30 minutes of going to bed
____ I sleep soundly throughout the night

Total for section #4 _____

#5 Social Connection – A Social Life is Life Support
____ I have enough friends to feel well connected socially
____ I seldom feel lonely
____ I maintain intimate emotional connection with others
____ I find time to participate in hobbies I enjoy just for fun
____ I have social interactions outside of work or family
____ I laugh often and experience joy throughout the day

Total for section #5 = _____

6 Brain Training – Cognitive Fitness
____ I seldom find myself multitasking
____ I maintain focus during the day
____ I feel mentally challenged on a regular basis
____ I have recently learned a new skill (language, art, etc)
____ I actively seek out challenging conversations with others
____ I have a strong sense of purpose in my life that I connect with frequently during the day

Total for section #6 = _____

Interpreting Your Results

It is important to note that there are no "good" or "bad" scores for this assessment. I designed this tool to help identify where to focus your time and energy if you want to see the most significant changes as you start your training program. If you find yourself running out of ink or needing to sharpen your pencil after making so many checkmarks, congratulations! On the other hand, if you didn't need to pick up your pen or pencil at all, do not panic. You are not alone. Although these concepts are simple in theory, being able to do all of them in the midst of a busy schedule is incredibly difficult. For all of us. The key to becoming *SHARP* is to take this process one small step at a time. Each new practice that you incorporate into your daily routine will make a big difference, and over time you will find yourself moving on to more advanced strategies that fully unleash the potential of your brain.

Realizing I run the risk of sounding a bit "motivational" here, please keep in mind that "A journey of a thousand miles begins with a single step" (Lao-tzu). After completing the assessment you may choose the area that needs the most work, or the one that you feel most confident you can make changes to quickly. You may want to focus on the area that you believe will give you the most return on your investment right away. As we go through the next section, I will identify specific strategies within each area of the assessment to make it simple to put a training plan in place.

STEP TWO
Understand Brain Basics

Navigating Neuroplasticity (for Normal People)

The term neuroplasticity may sound complicated, but the concept is simple. Neuro = brain. Plasticity = adaptability. Put the two together and you have an "adaptable brain." Considering that we can continue to change how we think and act throughout our lifespan, the idea of having an adaptable brain would seem to be common knowledge. Yet up until a few decades ago the brain was thought to be hardwired from a very early age. Experts assumed that specific areas of the brain were responsible for specific functions and that these could not be changed.

Although early research pioneers would challenge this assumption, most people believed that the brain was pretty much set once we reached adulthood. Look at a diagram of a brain, and you'll see certain areas zoned for movement of particular parts of the body, certain areas for thinking, memory and judgment, and others for hearing and vision. The thought was that if you were to damage a particular area of the brain, you would lose the ability to perform that function. Case closed.

Well, not exactly. Over the past two decades, radical studies have demonstrated that after a traumatic event such as injury or a stroke, parts of the brain that were supposed to control one element of our functioning could actually be recruited to take over for another. For example, individuals who became deaf after brain trauma showed more activity in the area of the brain that controls visual function and displayed a heightened sense of peripheral vision. Stroke victims who lost the ability to control one side of their body actually regained use after the brain was given the time and stimulus to adapt. New scanning technology proved that brain function wasn't hardwired after all.

It is beyond the scope of this book to go through all of the studies and the exact science behind neuroplasticity, but if you are interested in learning more (and I would highly recommend it because it's absolutely fascinating[1,2,3]), I have listed some of my favorite books and websites on this topic in the resources section at the end of Part Three. Instead, I want to focus on grasping the overall idea of neuroplasticity and the impact it can have on our daily lives. Most importantly, I want to give you the tools to help maximize the return on your investment once you start training, and maintaining, your brain.

In my work as a speaker and a coach, I've found that one of the best ways to explain a complex concept is to tell a story that helps simplify it. When things get too technical, our minds quickly become clouded with ideas that really don't have a big impact on what we're trying to achieve. Once things start to feel complicated, our brain quickly realizes that the effort just to understand will require a major energy investment, and if there are other things that need our attention (as there always are), we just can't take in the new information. Trust me, this happens to me all the time! On the other hand, if it's a story we can related to from a big-picture perspective, then understanding the complicated concept seems much more worthwhile, and we can focus on doing what's necessary to make that knowledge work for us.

The (Super Simplified) Story of "Brain Change"

Imagine you are the first to discover a new area of land. The very first. Picture a field covered with all sorts of overgrowth such as brush and weeds. I think about all the blackberry fields I used to play around growing up, and how challenging it was to navigate them when it was time to actually pick the berries (or retrieve a foul ball from our Wiffle ball game).

Now imagine that you need to get across the field in order to determine if there are usable resources on the other side. Maybe fresh water. Wild boar for dinner. Whatever it might be. The first time you try to clear your way across the field, it's a ton of work. You might even get hurt (if you're dealing with blackberry bushes, at least, and I have the scars to prove it). But eventually you plow your way across the rugged terrain and discover that there is a wonderful lake on the other side that will be helpful as you start to make your new home.

Next, imagine you have to repeat this same process over and over again, trying to get fresh water. Most likely you will use the path you already cleared, unless you discover a shortcut that might be easier. As you continue this process again and again, the path gets clearer and you are able to get to the lake more quickly, using less energy along the way.

Up until age 11 (or thereabouts), our brains navigate a field similar to this newly explored territory. We are born with more than 100 billion brain cells (for perspective, that is about 10 times the number of stars in the entire Milky Way and about 20 times the number of people on the planet). When we are born, we have approximately the same number of brain cells that we will have as an adult, although connections will continue to develop quickly during infancy and childhood before leveling off later in life. In fact, by age 3, a child's brain has formed about 1,000 trillion connections – about twice as many as adults have (and a heck of a lot more energy to keep us running after them).

As we enter into adolescence we begin a process of neural "pruning" to eliminate unnecessary connections. While that may sound depressing, think about how active your mind is right now and imagine what would happen if you retained all of the information and experiences you've been exposed to over your life. Talk about system overload!

During this pruning process, we have to do a lot of navigating through uncharted territory. As we clear more paths, the ones we don't clear begin to atrophy, making them more difficult to use in the future. Kind of like an unused pathway that weeds quickly take control over, you have to work harder to re-establish the route. As we get older, our options may decrease in size, but our ability to create new pathways is still there.

What's more, we have the ability to use more effective tools as we get older to help clear paths quicker and more effectively. (By the way, those tools are exactly what will be described later in this book). Assuming we are all quite a bit past our prime clearing age of 11, we need all the tools we can get if we want to create pathways that will be more efficient and effective at helping us accomplish the things that are important to us.

This story of clearing paths and making them easier for us to navigate is a very simplified metaphor for how we create new ways of thinking, establish new habits, and even change behaviors. The continued overgrowth of the paths we don't choose is part of the reason it's difficult to "teach an old dog new tricks."

I'm going to take this one step further. Let's assume we've cleared several pathways to do the things we need to do but allowed the others to grow weeds. Over time, the pathways we have created become easier to use, requiring less effort or energy. Just like clearing out a path in a field, the more we walk on that path the clearer it becomes, the more packed down the brush gets, and eventually we may have a dirt road, clear of any clutter. With more time and experience, we can actually add gravel and begin to pave the road, based on how much we practice and how we live our lives.

For example, we all know exercise is good for us. It makes us smarter, happier, and healthier. But you may not realize that exercising our body, and our brain, is a bit like throwing down concrete on our mental pathways. As Harvard professor John Ratey describes in his groundbreaking book, *Spark: The Revolutionary New Science of Exercise and the Brain* (a must read in my opinion), aerobic exercise stimulates a chemical (BDNF or brain derived neurotrophic factor, in case you were wondering) that acts like "miracle grow" to brain cells.[4] We can also literally exercise the brain and get similar effects. When we consistently challenge our brains, we add structural support to the pathways, making it even easier for us to think and act in the ways we want to.

It sounds almost counterintuitive, but this structural support doesn't weigh us down. This "concrete in the brain," known as myelin sheath, is a fatty tissue that makes connections between brain cells more effective and efficient. But because it's live tissue, it has to be maintained, just like we have to maintain any part of our body. We have to use it, or we lose it. So if we stop repeating a particular path, it will start to become more challenging to navigate — re-growing some of those difficult "weeds," so to speak—and will make the clearing process more challenging once again.

The strategies discussed in the next few chapters are tools that will enable you to clear solid pathways between the brain cells that need to communicate effectively for you to think and behave the way you want to. The key is clearing the paths we want to be using regularly and letting the ones we don't want to use become less desirable, or more "weedy."

Survival Mode

Just like the rest of our body, the brain is designed in a way that is best suited for our survival. Because we require energy to survive, our control center will move us toward the path of least resistance so that we can hold on to as much energy as possible. Looking back on the history of mankind, there have been times when energy available from food has run out. In these cases, survival may have been in doubt, so the more people had and the less they needed, the better off they were. It makes perfect sense, in certain circumstances. The problem today is that our automatic-pilot mode — designed to help us survive — is making it nearly impossible to have a healthy lifestyle.

Cognitive scientists frame the dilemma this way: We have two different processing systems in the brain, the automated system (or auto-brain) and the reflective system (or thinking brain). In times of danger, the automated system takes over and allows us to act quickly, which is important when we need to react to a threat or run away from danger. Don't think, just do.

When we are faced with decisions that require more thought, the reflective system is in charge. It takes the time it needs to make the best decision for the current circumstances. Judgment, learning, evaluating, feeling, and emotions are all part of the reflective system. For survival purposes, our auto-brain has to be ready to take charge at any moment. There are occasions when trying to debate multiple choices could leave us dead in our tracks, such as a fire rapidly burning through our home. Times like this call for an immediate response, which can be like a knee-jerk reaction to a particular situation.

Managing Our Monkey Brain

When we find ourselves slipping into survival mode, it can feel pretty chaotic. Consider what happens when you've gone too long without eating, haven't had a good night sleep in awhile, or haven't seen the sun in days. You might not feel quite like yourself. At these times I like to remind myself that my "monkey brain" has taken over. I happen to be a huge monkey fan, so I instantly get a big smile on my face. Monkeys always seem to be in a pretty good mood and are usually playing around, acting silly. So the initial reaction to thinking about something called our "monkey brain" just makes me laugh (and we'll talk about how important laughter is to staying healthy in an upcoming chapter). On a more serious note, there is another important reason to consider how the monkey brain responds differently than other parts of our brain, and when that can be detrimental.

Our brain can be separated into three sections: lizard, monkey, and human. The "lizard brain" is found at the base of the organ; it contains the cerebellum and brain stem. Lizards have only these elements of the brain, which control our most basic instincts. The next part, the "monkey brain," includes the majority of our tissue and controls more complex tasks as well as emotions. Most mammals lead with their "monkey brain," which fuels our most basic responses to fear and desire.

The most advanced part, the "human brain," consists of the outer layer surrounding the "monkey brain." This area allows for logical, emotionless thought, such as delayed gratification. By using our "human brain" we are able to think through our responses, rather than just reacting. But when we are faced with threats to our system, we don't have time to stop and analyze what's going on. During these times we are glad to have our "lizard" and "monkey" brains to quickly get us to safety, employing our fight-or-flight response.

Because we have so many things going on at one time, when we multitask we can easily find ourselves using our "monkey brain." We make mindless decisions that may end up causing serious problems with important tasks, or even worse, with important relationships. Next time you find yourself trying to do a million things at once and getting irritable or grumpy with someone you care about, remind yourself that you're using your "monkey brain" – and work on acting more like a human. (Although I'd caution against calling your spouse a monkey when he or she is acting up, it might be a good code word for times when you feel like the other person isn't giving you the full attention you really want.)

We Are Creatures of Habit

There are two reasons why this concept is critical to our brain-training program. First, we need to keep in mind that many of our thoughts and responses are generated in our auto-brain. They do not come from a place of thoughtful consideration, or mindfulness. Many times people get caught up in thinking that these random thoughts generated by our auto-brain represent who they are. In reality, our thoughts often pop up out of nowhere. Second, and most important, we have the ability to train our auto-brain to respond differently.

There are many examples of this idea in sports and other types of competition. Skilled chess players and elite athletes have trained themselves to analyze complex situations quickly in order to respond in the best way, as fast as possible. Through practice, these superstars are able to train elements of their brain that normally would be part of the reflective, thoughtful system to react within a matter of seconds.

As a competitive softball pitcher I spent dozens of hours each week practicing my ability to throw a ball underhand as fast as I could. But that wasn't my only task. The speed of the ball heading to the batter seemed slow compared to the way it jumped off the swinging bat, often heading right back in my direction. Years of training helped me develop exceptional eye-hand coordination so that I could protect myself from line drives hit back at me (at least most of the time).

We can see plenty of examples of our auto-brain in action throughout our daily routines. Think of all of the things you do during the day that you could almost do in your sleep (and maybe sometimes you do). Get up, turn the coffee pot on, brush your teeth, shower, get dressed, drive to work, walk to your office... did you really have to pay much attention to get all those things done? Because our auto-brain requires a very small amount of energy, it's always going to be the preferred way of processing information and facilitating behavior.

Our auto-brain is not a bad thing. It's actually a great thing, as long as we are aware of how it functions so that we can be sure it's moving us in the right direction. Sometimes we miss things because we assume we know what's coming next. Our brain assesses situations constantly, making interpretations that are often accurate but always based on perception. When we function in auto-brain mode, there are a lot of things that can be missed.

Here is an example of how your auto-brain works:

Aoccdrnig to a research sduty at Cmabrigde Uinervtisy, it deosn't mttaer in what order the ltteers in a word are, the only iprmoetnt thing is that the frist and lsat ltteer be in the rghit pclae. The rset can be a total mses and you can still raed it wouthit porbelms. Tish is bcuseae the human mind does not raed ervey lteter by istlef, but the word as a wlohe.

People are often surprised by how easily they can read the paragraph above (try typing it… that's very strange, too, because your brain quickly anticipates what the word should say and automatically wants to   correct it.) Because our brain focuses primarily on patterns and is able to make assumptions, even gibberish can make sense as long as certain patterns remain consistent (which, in this case, means the first and last letters are accurate).

Remember, our brain wants to conserve energy for possible threats during the day, so it always prefers automatic pilot mode. In *The Power of Full Engagement*, co-author Jim Loehr, one of my mentors, proposes that approximately 95% of human behavior happens in this automated state of mind, while only 5% is conscious, self-regulated behavior.[5]

What's critical to understand is that when our thoughts or behaviors become part of our 95% automatic processing system, they are pretty easy to maintain. They don't require a lot of energy. We would call these our habits, and the good ones are ingrained so that we can rely on them to support us. But not all of our habits are good (obviously), and those darn bad habits are very difficult to change because they happen automatically after years of training them to do so, whether we are trying to or not.

Everything we do in life has a training effect. If you find yourself grabbing fast food on a regular basis, you will soon feel pulled in that direction when you start to feel hungry. Stay up late several nights working (or writing a book), and you will train your brain to see this as the norm, making falling asleep at a decent hour much more challenging.

Unless we consciously make an effort to change bad habits our brains keep these pathways "well-paved," and we keep repeating them. The brain training principles discussed in the next few sections will help you consciously change the focus of your mental energy to develop more supportive habits that are easy to maintain. With such an amazing operating system that can help us automate processes in our life, why not train our brain to move us in the right direction and make our auto-brain our ultimate resource?

Changing Pathways — Creating a Better Auto-brain

In order to strengthen the pathways we find helpful and make the others less appealing, we must invest time and energy in optimizing both the structure and functions of our brain. To create more positive pathways in the brain, we need specific materials and just the right tools. Consider the *SYNERGY Fab 5* health fundamentals described in Part Two as providing the foundation of your *SHARP* brain, with each dimension adding a critical element to the structure of your cognitive fitness.

The specific brain training strategies in Part Three will provide the tools to help mold and shape your brain to run smoothly, taking you in the direction of your goals. This will essentially upgrade your brain, preparing it to maximize your performance, enhance your resilience, and optimize your mental endurance.

"My employer is paying for the surgery. I'm having a speed bump installed between my brain and my mouth."

STEP 3
Create a Healthy Foundation

"To keep the body in good health is a duty…otherwise we shall not be able to keep our mind strong and clear".

Buddha, circa 500 BC

The SYNERGY Fab 5

Before we look at how to improve cognitive fitness, we need to make sure to set the right foundation. This is critical to making sure that the training we do is effective. In a sense, it's like using the right materials to make certain that the work you do will take hold and last over time, building a solid foundation. Each of these elements help to create the right brain chemistry, including the optimal amount of brain chemicals to help neurons communicate most effectively and stay strong and resilient over time.

Brain health is currently one of the top health-related concerns of aging populations, according to the Centers for Disease Control and studies by the AARP. While brain diseases like Alzheimer's and other forms of dementia take center stage when we talk about cognitive decline, it can often prove difficult to determine in an elderly individual if they actually have Alzheimer's disease or are suffering from other types of cognitive impairment.

In fact, my grandfather was diagnosed with Alzheimer's disease – a serious blow to my family – only to later find out that his cognitive impairments were being caused by a medication mismatch. While it was great to know he was free of Alzheimer's disease and would most likely live a longer, healthier life than we initially imagined, I couldn't help but wonder how many other individuals are misdiagnosed, either for the better or the worse, because of the multitude of influences on our brain health and cognitive functioning.

Late-life cognitive impairment may be a result of multiple hits to the brain from a variety of factors, including medical issues such as heart disease and hypertension, diabetes, or head trauma. It can also be a result of situational issues such as poor diet, obesity, sedentary lifestyle, chronic stress, lack of sleep, or loneliness.

While the pieces of the puzzle continue to be discovered and placed into a bigger, more understandable picture, there are several sure-thing strategies that experts agree will provide us with the best brain environment, or foundation. Ultimately, these strategies will keep us healthy and happy, with optimal cognitive functioning, for as long as possible.

To tackle each of the lifestyle elements that are within our control, I created the *SYNERGY Fab 5* – the most important rules to follow when your goal is optimal health, happiness, and performance of the body and mind. Each component has a synergistic effect when combined with the others.

GLASBERGEN
Copyright 2008 by Randy Glasbergen.

"What fits your busy schedule better, exercising 30 minutes a day or being dead 24 hours a day?"

RULE #1
Food is Fuel
"Let food be thy medicine." – Hippocrates

How we choose to fuel our body might be the most important choice we make when it comes to our brainpower. In fact, the glucose we get from the foods we eat is the primary source of fuel for our brain. Though it only takes up about 3% of our total body mass, our brain utilizes approximately 20% of the glucose and oxygen we consume. In order to keep this energy-demanding organ functioning at its best, it is critical that we keep glucose levels steady throughout the day, and that we boost our brain health with foods that enhance and nourish both the structure and function of our brain.

There are three key strategies to optimizing nutrition for brain health. First, eat small amounts regularly throughout the day. Second, eat in a way that balances blood sugar at each meal and snack. And third, maximize the brain-building benefits of eating by choosing the "power foods."

These are the same strategies I would recommend if this book were about feeling more energetic, enhancing performance in physical training or an athletic event, improving heart health, decreasing the risk of developing diabetes, or managing weight. The fundamentals are always the same, and they are the most important strategies to focus on as you develop your *SHARP* nutrition plan. Following these simple guidelines will get you far in your journey towards your health and performance goals, whatever they may be. In fact, I'd say the fundamentals make up at least 85–90% of the equation, no matter what you're trying to improve with your diet.

You will notice that I'm calling these suggestions "strategies", and this is intentional. They are goals you want to strive for, but not that you're expected to do 100% of the time. In order to have a sustainable nutrition plan, it's important to avoid making it overly rigid. Otherwise, your tendency, and this is true for all of us, will be to rebel against the rules or follow an all-or-nothing mentality of being either "on" or "off" a diet. If you are able to use these strategies regularly, the occasional indulgence won't feel like you just fell off of an imaginary wagon. Be strategic about how you eat most of the time, and you'll be on a great path toward a healthy, happy, and fit brain.

The recommendations below are simple to grasp, but they are not easy to implement (otherwise we'd already be doing all of them). In the first part of this section, we will cover the "what" – specifically, what you should be doing with your nutrition plan for optimal brain health. Second, we will talk about the "why" – so you can understand exactly why these simple strategies are so important, and the overall impact they will have on your brain and your body. Finally, I will discuss the "how" – important ways that you can use your brain to improve your diet, while you use your diet to improve your brain.

Key Strategy #1 – Eat small portions, frequently

In order to keep glucose levels consistent and avoid dipping in to "survival mode" throughout the day, it is critical to eat in a way that keeps you in your optimal blood sugar (glucose) range. A lack of glucose starves the brain of energy, while too much can cause system overload. In fact, science shows that insulin spikes may be quite damaging to brain cells, which could be why some brain experts consider Alzheimer's disease to be "Type 3 diabetes."[1] (This is just one of many areas of focus in current Alzheimer's research, so the specific connection is still being evaluated. For more information, visit www.alz.org.) While there is no exact ideal blood glucose level or one-size-fits-all approach to accomplishing this optimal state, a good rule of thumb is to eat something that causes you to feel satisfied, not full, approximately every 3–4 hours during the day.

Determining what this eating plan looks like can be challenging. In one of the "Blue Zones," Buettner describes how the Okinawan people follow a philosophy of eating in moderation, "hari hachi bu," or eating to the point you feel

80% full.[2] Because it can take up to 20 minutes for your brain to recognize satiety signals from the body, and because we tend to eat so darn fast these days, aiming for 80% can be a great strategy to end up on target. For most people, this equates to about 4 handfuls of food at meals (1 handful of grains, 1 handful of protein, and 2 handfuls of fruits and vegetables), and about 100–200 calories at each snack. (For more individualized recommendations, please visit www.eatright.org to locate a registered dietitian in your area).

Key Strategy #2 – Eat balanced

To make sure our glucose levels aren't spiking or crashing, it also important to have the right combination of nutrients – complex carbohydrate, lean protein, and healthy fat. For an ideal brain-healthy plate, I recommend a 25/25/50 split of foods to keep blood sugar levels balanced and maximize the amount of "power foods" you get in your meal, primarily from fruits and vegetables that have brain-protecting nutrients.

It is important to have a variety of energy sources in your food: quick energy providers in carbohydrates and slower sources of energy in fat and protein. As living plant sources, fruits and vegetables develop protective phytochemicals called antioxidants to help them avoid environmental damage. Upon consumption, these nutrients can also help protect our body and brain from damage that occurs as a byproduct of our normal metabolic process.

Key Strategy #3 – Eat foods with high nutritional value

For optimal brain health, focus on maximizing the number of beneficial foods you eat and minimizing those that may be harmful. A recent report by the National Institutes of Health stated that, among all of the evidence reviewed, only two strategies were shown to have good support for their ability to decrease the development of Alzheimer's and cognitive decline – cognitive training, which we will discuss in part three, and a Mediterranean diet.[3] This way of eating is based on commonly consumed cuisine in areas of the Mediterranean, such as Spain, Italy, and Greece.

The Mediterranean diet includes foods that are excellent at keeping the body functioning at its best. These foods offer a balance of nutrients, including whole grain carbohydrates, lean protein, and healthy fat. Eating such foods stabilizes blood glucose, providing a consistent and stable source of fuel for the body and brain. The quality of nutrients in these foods also has a high impact. You get monounsaturated fat, omega-3 fat, lean protein, fiber, and many vitamins, minerals, and other protective nutrients such as antioxidants and polyphenols. At the same time, the Mediterranean diet decreases the focus on foods that may be harmful to our health, such as saturated fat, trans fat, and highly processed carbohydrates.

SHARP Science – In a study of two thousand Manhattan residents averaging 76 years of age, those eating a Mediterranean diet had a 68 percent lower risk of developing Alzheimer's.[4]

Power Foods

Below you will find a list of "power foods" that will help boost your brain. Aim for a plant-based, Mediterranean diet and minimize things that may be damaging, including processed foods, saturated and trans fats, alcohol in excess, and added sugar.

- Fish (or fish oil supplements)
- Poultry and other lean meats
- Beans and legumes
- Eggs (including yolks)
- Low fat milk, cheese, and yogurt
- Nuts and seeds: almonds, cashews, walnuts, hazelnuts, Brazil nuts, peanuts, sunflower seeds, sesame seeds, flax seed, peanut butter, almond butter
- Olives, olive oil, avocado
- Whole grain bread, cereal, and pasta
- Fruits (especially berries), and dark colored fruit juices (such as concord grape and pomegranate)
- Vegetables (especially leafy greens like spinach and lettuces, red bell peppers, broccoli, and broccoli sprouts)
- Wine (in moderation)
- Coffee and tea (in moderation)
- Spices, especially turmeric, ginger, cinnamon, saffron and garlic

Power foods make your brain work better by offering key building blocks that strengthen its structure. Some of the most critical nutrients for the brain are listed below.

Omega-3 fatty acids: The brain is a fatty organ. Therefore, one of the most important nutrients to consume is long-chain omega 3 fatty acids, which help maintain flexibility, nourish cell membranes, and decrease inflammation. Omega-3 fatty acids are essential for brain growth and development in childhood and throughout our lifespan. They are involved in many brain functions, keep cell membranes flexible in order to promote connections between cells, and have an antioxidant and anti-inflammatory impact on both the brain and the body. Research shows that diets low in omega-3 can alter the chemical balance in the brain, potentially leading to mood disorders such as anxiety and depression.

Another fatty acid, omega-6, works in partnership with omega-3. Omega-6 triggers an inflammatory response, which is necessary for immune functioning, while omega-3 keeps inflammation from getting out of hand. For optimal health and functioning, there is an ideal ratio of omega-3 to omega-6 fatty acids (approximately 1:3). One of the challenges with our modern diet is that we consume too many omega-6s, which cause an unhealthy ratio in the brain and body (closer to 1:20). Vegetable oils (especially corn) and meat from animals fed primarily corn meal (as opposed to their grass-fed counterparts) are high in omega-6 fatty acids.

Omega-3 fatty acids have a well deserved reputation for many health benefits, including reducing depression, anxiety, and heart disease, stabilizing mood, and maintaining memory. The best omega-3s, called docosahexaenoic acid (DHA) and eicosapentaenoic acid (EPA), can be found in fatty fish (salmon, mackerel, tuna, etc.), fish oil, or algae. We can get another kind of omega-3 fat, called alpha linolenic acid (ALA), from nuts, seeds and grains, but the ALA found in these foods has not been found to be as beneficial to the body or the brain as DHA and EPA. Some ALA is converted to DHA, but the conversion rate is quite small (studies vary, but most seem to estimate about 20–30%). (For more information on omega-3 fatty acids, see *The Omega-3 Connection* by Dr. Andrew Stoll.)

Because blood flow is so critical to brainpower, what is good for the heart is good for the brain. The American Heart Association recommends that patients with cardiovascular disease consume about 1,000 mg of omega-3s (specifically, combined DHA+EPA) per day; those without documented CHD should eat a variety of oily fish at least twice a week to provide about 500 mg of this omega-3 combination daily.[5]

Monounsaturated fat: Most people have heard about the benefits of omega-3, but you may not realize that other types of fat also help develop strong connections in the brain. Monounsaturated fats found in plant sources such as olives and olive oil, nuts and seeds, and avocado help produce the good type of cholesterol in the bloodstream (HDL or high density lipoprotein), which keeps blood flow running smoothly.

Lean protein: Protein is necessary for the body to maintain healthy metabolism and to repair and rebuild lean tissue in the body. Amino acids found in protein contribute to the production of enzymes and antibodies, and are critical to healthy immune functioning. As part of a healthy diet, lean protein helps stabilize blood sugar because it is slower to break down into usable energy.

Fiber: Dietary fiber is beneficial for maintaining healthy blood flow, eliminating toxic waste from the system, and improving feelings of satiety, or fullness, which can aid with weight loss or weight management. The average Western diet only provides about 10–12 grams of fiber per day, but the recommendation for adults is closer to 25–35 grams a day. Aim for fiber-rich foods such as beans and lentils, fruits and vegetables, and whole grains, and supplement as needed.

Flavanoids and other antioxidants: Flavanoids are nutrients found in plant sources that have antioxidant properties. Upon consumption, these nutrients can also help protect our body and brain from oxidative damage caused by free radicals, a normal byproduct of our energy-producing metabolic process. Fruits and vegetables are our primary sources of flavanoids, but there several other options. For example, the flavanoid found in cocoa is said to help increase blood flow to the brain. Dark chocolate also releases dopamine, an important neurochemical for brain health and development. Other foods rich in antioxidants include coffee, tea, wine, and spices.

Vitamin D: Often called the sunshine vitamin, vitamin D is well known for its importance in the absorption of calcium. Scientists have recently discovered that there are many other health conditions related to low vitamin D levels. Recent research suggests that vitamin D impacts elements of our immune system, blood pressure, and cell growth, and may be connected to a host of diseases such as multiple sclerosis, cancer, and heart disease.[2] Vitamin D levels have also been associated with cognitive function in older adults. In a study of elders receiving home care, researchers found that only 35% of the participants had sufficient vitamin D levels, and those with adequate vitamin D performed better on cognitive aptitude tests than those who were deficient.[6]

Our bodies manufacture vitamin D when our skin is exposed to sunlight. Moderate sun exposure on the arms and legs for 5—30 minutes, depending on season and latitude, can enhance vitamin D levels. While our skin has the ability to synthesize large amounts of vitamin D, overexposure to the sun can cause skin cancer; therefore, anything above low-to-moderate exposure is not recommended.[7]

Vitamin D is fat-soluble, which means it is stored in the liver and fatty tissues, and is eliminated at a slower rate than water soluble vitamins (other fat soluble vitamins include A, E, and K). Vitamin D is not naturally abundant in food. Dietary sources include fish, eggs, and cod liver oil. There are also foods that are fortified with the vitamin, such as certain grains and milk. Because food sources of vitamin D are limited, a vitamin D supplement may be recommended. Although there is still some debate about how much vitamin D we really need, most experts recommend at least 1,000 IU daily.[8] Your doctor can order a blood test to determine your level and advise you on the right amount for you.

Magnesium: Recent studies have shown that elevating brain magnesium may enhance learning and memory. It has been estimated that half the population of industrialized countries has a magnesium deficit, which increases with aging. Magnesium is required for more than 300 biochemical reactions in the body, including heart, muscle, and nerve functioning. In an animal study, an increase in magnesium was correlated with increased strength of brain connections in the hippocampus, which controls long-term memory and spatial navigation.[9]

Dietary sources of magnesium include beans and legumes, nuts and seeds, whole grains, and vegetables. Magnesium supplements are also available.

Choline: A vitamin-like compound, choline is used by the body to produce acetylcholine, one of the most important memory neurotransmitters in the brain. Choline is essential for breaking down fat to produce energy, and it is involved in the movement of cholesterol in the body, possibly helping to keep cholesterol deposits from forming in blood vessels. Diets that are too low in fat represent a threat to acetylcholine levels. With insufficient acetylcholine, cell membranes become brittle and fall away.

The primary dietary sources of choline are animal foods such as beef and eggs. Choline can be found in some plant foods, particularly soybeans and wheat germ. It can also be found in supplement form in soy lecithin.

Based on animal studies, choline may treat or possibly prevent dementia. Individuals who suffer from dementia often have lower-than-normal levels of acetycholine, which affects both memory and muscles. It is believed that choline supplementation may improve symptoms associated with dementia by helping the body to increase and maintain levels of acetylcholine. While this is a current area of research in Alzheimer's and other types of dementia, at this point no human studies have tested whether choline may actually be beneficial for treating cognitive decline or disease.

Folate: Whole grains such as wheat bran, wheat germ, brown rice, oatmeal, and barley have high amounts of folate, as do asparagus, beans, oranges, and strawberries. According to the Nun Study, low levels of folic acid in the blood were associated with atrophy of the cerebral cortex, which could lead to an early decline in cognitive functioning.[10]

In addition to eating a healthy diet, most health professionals generally recommend that you consume a *multivitamin* on a daily basis. These supplements are meant to balance out any nutrient deficiencies you have. But keep in mind this is one area where more is not necessarily better. If you're lacking key nutrients (and many of us are based on the quality of our food), then covering some extra ground with supplements is a great idea. But take too many vitamins, and you may find yourself experiencing complications as minor as some digestive discomfort or trouble sleeping or serious enough to land you in the hospital.

Don't spend extra money on the fancy varieties, either. A recent *Consumer Reports* study evaluated both generic and more expensive brands of multivitamins and found that they were pretty much equal in performance.[11] Some of the cheaper generic brands actually performed better than the wallet busters.

Fuel Your Brain

By utilizing the three key strategies described above, you optimize the performance of your body for the purpose of assisting the development of your brain. We have already discussed the importance of controlling blood sugar to provide the brain with consistent fuel and to keep insulin at a healthy level. We do this by eating small amounts regularly during the day, in a well-balanced manner. We also want to maximize the healthy nutrients in the diet to make sure the brain is getting enough of what it needs, and not too much of what it doesn't.

In this next section, we will discuss some additional ways that these simple strategies impact the brain by boosting the way that other parts of the body function. But first, let's look at why eating this way is so important, and why it can prove to be so challenging.

The Evolution of Nutrition

Energy is our most valuable resource, and we get energy into the body by eating food. Because humans have experienced energy deficits throughout our history, our brain and body are always a bit on edge, wondering if we may run out of fuel again sometime soon. While a famine seems incredibly unlikely, our brain still wants to guarantee that there is never an energy shortage. So it drives us to eat as much as we can when we can, and to move as little as possible when it's not critical. Eating small portions frequently and moving consistently throughout the day go against our energy conservation mode, making it very difficult to stick with those habits even when we know we should.

When we give the brain any indication that we might soon experience an energy shortage, our body quickly goes into conservation mode. Metabolism slows down and appetite goes up. We crave quick energy sources like processed carbohydrates and sugar. This natural process would be critical if indeed we were stranded on a deserted island without food, but it's not helpful if we're trying our best to eat in a healthy way. The key to making all of this work in harmony? Convince the brain that there is no food shortage by providing it with the nutrients it requires on a consistent basis. But go too long without eating, and the brain interprets that as a famine. Eat junk (foods low in nutritional value), and your body still thinks it's starving, which results in more cravings.

The first reason we need to follow the three key nutrition strategies is to make sure our brain is getting glucose and other nutrients it needs consistently throughout the day so that it can be adequately fueled (not too little, not too much). This approach will keep us out of conservation mode and able to produce the quality and quantity of energy we need to keep us fully fueled throughout the day. Eating this way also helps reduce stress, as inconsistent meals and the fear of upcoming famine are quite stressful to the brain and body.

Of course, eating well helps reduce stress, and reducing stress helps us eat well. Keep in mind that stress management plays a huge role in this equation, because stress hormones also trigger a response that changes our body's metabolism for the worse. Similar to a food shortage, any stress on our system (physical or psychological) causes a shift in metabolism, glucose regulation, and cognitive functioning.

Healthy Heart = Healthy Brain

First, because circulation of glucose and oxygen is critical to keep the brain fueled appropriately, it is important to make sure that you eat in a way that is optimal for blood flow. This means keeping arteries clear from excess cholesterol, triglycerides, and inflammation. According to the Alzheimer's Association, what is good for the heart is good for the brain.

A Mediterranean diet consisting of lean protein, whole grains, and healthy fat will promote heart health. That means you'll help your heart and your brain by eating in a way that keeps unhealthy cholesterol at bay and decreases inflammation. The tools: healthy fats found in foods like nuts, seeds, and olive oil, omega-3 fatty acids in fish, fiber in beans and lentils, and antioxidants and other phytochemicals in fruits, vegetables, wine, coffee, tea, and spices. To keep triglycerides in a healthy range it is important to limit or avoid processed carbohydrates (such as white bread, white rice, crackers, pretzels, and chips) and added sugars, and to keep alcohol consumption to a moderate amount (1-2 servings a day).

Maintain a Healthy Weight

Many experts have suggested that a healthy weight may be essential to a healthy brain. According to *Think Smart* author Richard Restak, obesity is more often associated with cognitive impairment than age, gender, education, or IQ.[12] A bigger waistline has also been associated with a smaller brain. A study at the University of Pittsburgh School of Medicine showed that the brain of an overweight person appeared 16 years older than the brain of a normal weight person.[13] Results from a new imaging study reveal that, on average, obese subjects had 8% lower brain volume than normal-weight subjects, and overweight subjects had 4% lower brain volume.

In multiple studies body mass index (BMI) has been negatively correlated with brain atrophy; in other words, the higher the BMI, the more the brain becomes damaged as a result of the aging process. Study investigator Cyrus Raji said in a statement, "that could mean that exercising, eating right, and keeping weight under control can maintain brain health with aging and potentially lower the risk for Alzheimer's and other dementias."[14] In addition, the negative health behaviors associated with obesity are also associated with heart disease and diabetes, which negatively impact the flow of oxygen and glucose to the brain.

> ***SHARP Science:*** A study at the Karolinska Institute in Stockholm found that participants who had been overweight in middle age had an 80% higher risk of being diagnosed with dementia in later life. Obese people, those having a body mass index (BMI) of 30 or above, had an almost four times higher risk of dementia.[15]

Because BMI only takes into account weight and height, it is important to keep an eye on your body fat percentage, which may give you a more accurate measure of your health risk. Some people are short with a large amount of muscle tissue, while others are tall and appear lean, but have too much fat to be considered healthy. Excellent resources for calculating body fat include the Bod Pod (www.bodpod.com), underwater weighing (seldom available outside of university or clinical settings), bioelectrical impedance (hand held devices or scales), or calipers (the pinch-an-inch method, which needs to be done by someone who is well trained in order to be accurate.)

The Mind-Body-Weight Connection

Each of the *SYNERGY Fab 5* elements follows somewhat of a chicken-egg phenomenon: Which should come first? If you do the healthy practices recommended in this book, your mind will be sharper. Sharpen your mind, and you will be more able to stick with the strategies that benefit both your body and your mind. When it comes to eating right, the mind-body connection is critical to keep in mind.

When I meet with clients who want to lose weight, they always want to focus on the logistics of their program. "Tell me what to eat and I'll do it," they say. But we all know if it were that easy, we wouldn't be in the midst of a national obesity epidemic. It is not figuring out what to do that is the challenge; it's figuring out how to actually do it—and stick with it.

Studies have shown that all diets work and no diets work. In the A-Z Weight Loss study, researchers found that all diets showed similar effectiveness when people were able to comply with the recommendations.[16] Unfortunately, only about 5% of people are able to maintain weight loss. Most actually end up gaining back their weight, and then some – leaving them in worse shape than they were before the diet. Usually this yo-yo effect also wreaks havoc on the metabolic system, making it more and more difficult to lose weight over time.

Because of my frustration with diet programs, I decided to do my doctoral research on the impact of stress on weight loss and weight management. According to many weight management experts I consulted for the project, an individual's use of coping skills is a critical factor in that person's ability to stay on a successful weight loss program. Although stress has proven to be detrimental to weight loss efforts, there has been little research on which stress management strategies are most effective at helping individuals build the coping skills they need to deal with stress effectively.

As expected, it was difficult to find quality studies that showed how to teach individuals to manage stress more successfully. In fact, when I evaluated the research, I looked at the most recent 100 articles on weight management and found that the majority of studies evaluated physical strategies for weight loss. Only a few studies examined the best strategies for other aspects of weight management – those dealing with the mental or emotional components.

Yet, ask anyone what he or she should be doing to lose weight when it comes to nutrition and exercise, and you will almost always find that people already know what works for them and what doesn't. The keys to sustainable weight management are learning to stick with the program and learning how to deal with life's challenges in healthier ways.

Use Your Brain to Take Care of Your Body

According to a study in the *American Journal of Clinical Nutrition*, successful dieters (those who have lost at least 30 pounds and kept it off) are more able to engage areas of their brain involved with will power and self-control than those who were obese or normal weight.[17] This indicates that being "cognitively fit" in key areas of the brain may be the solution for long-term weight management. Taking care of the brain is a critical part of successful, sustainable weight loss. The cognitive fitness strategies in Part Three will help you train your brain in a way that will help create healthy behavior change to support you in reaching your goals.

When it comes to losing weight and keeping it off, it is important to follow the time-tested strategies of eating small amounts frequently, eating balanced meals, and eating nutrient-rich foods as often as possible. Utilizing the strategies mentioned in the remaining *SYNERGY Fab 5* elements will also help to make your program sustainable by keeping both your body and your brain optimally fueled. Take care of your body, and your brain will benefit. Take care of your brain, and your body will benefit.

Summary:

1. Manage glucose levels by eating small, frequent, and balanced
2. Enjoy foods with high nutrient value the majority of the time (especially fruits, vegetables, and omega-3 fatty acids)
3. Limit brain drain by eating nutritious food whenever possible
4. Keep blood flow running smoothly (decrease blood fat and inflammation)
5. Maintain a healthy weight

(For Mediterranean diet inspired meals and snacks, see the resources section – p. 199.)

"If the brain is mostly made of fat,
then gaining weight in college
helps you get smarter!"

Rule #2
Activity is Activating
"Those who think they have not time for bodily exercise
will sooner or later have to find time for illness." –

Edward Stanley

Good circulation is critical to get glucose and oxygen to the
brain for energy. According to *Brain Rules* author John Medina,
after about 9 minutes and 59 seconds of sitting our brain thinks
it's vacation time.[1] The longer people sit, the higher their risk of
many health problems. A study published in the *American
Journal of Epidemiology* showed that among 123,000 adults
followed over 14 years, those who sat more than six hours a
day were at least 18 percent more likely to die than those who
sat less than three hours a day.[2]

There is no doubt that modern conveniences make life
easier in many ways. In fact, I'm pretty sure you can do just
about anything from the comfort of your couch. Shopping,
reading, watching movies, talking with friends, playing games,
ordering food, doing research, even dating can now be done
virtually, without having to move a muscle.

Yet, according to James Levine, a Mayo Clinic
endocrinologist and author of a paper called "Comfortable but
Deadly," the kinds of advances in technology that allow for
such conveniences may actually shorten your life.[3] He calls
sitting "the new smoking," stating that being seated for long
periods of time is hazardous to our health. "We were built to
stand, to move, to walk," he says. And we used to do all three
regularly. Experts estimate that our Paleolithic ancestors had to
walk 5–10 miles on an average day just to be able to eat. Levine
is so fanatical about not sitting at work that he walks at 1 mph
all day on a treadmill at his desk.[3] Simple physical activity such
as walking increases your breathing and heart rate, which
enhances blood flow, energy production, and waste removal.

Exercise stimulates the production of many different hormones necessary for cognitive functioning, in addition to changing the actual structure of the brain. For example, BDNF – our "miracle grow for the brain" – is boosted through aerobic exercise. A 2004 University of Illinois study found that people with high levels of aerobic fitness showed greater activation in key brain regions during performance of cognitive tasks, compared with their less fit counterparts.[4] Exercise also increases the amount and capacity of blood vessels in the brain. Unfortunately, despite all the people we think we see working hard in the gym, only about 5% of people even get the minimum amounts of exercise recommended for good health.

Remember, our survival instincts steer us to conserve energy – eat more, move less. In order to make physical activity something we move towards instead of away from, we have to train our brain to see movement as a benefit that's worth making the upfront energy investment. We have to spend a little to get a lot more.

Every Step Counts

When it comes to the performance of our brain, general activity may actually play a bigger role than formal exercise. There are many ways we can increase our general movement throughout the day: Avoid drive-thru joints, park further away, take the stairs instead of the elevator, use a headset and walk around when making calls, put your printer in another room, try a standing desk or countertop at least part of the day, or have walking one-on-one meetings at work.

The general movement you get throughout the day may be even more important than exercise when it comes to facilitating healthy circulation, and yet it takes a minimal time commitment and doesn't require a change of clothes (always keep walking shoes by your desk). Each morning look at your schedule and see if you can fit in more activity by planning ahead and scheduling breaks.

Exercise Strengthens the Brain

According to a large body of evidence, aerobic exercise increases and strengthens neuronal connections, increases the number of capillaries supplying glucose and oxygen to the brain, feeds the brain neurotropins (chemical messengers) that enhance growth and connections, and promotes new cell growth, or neurogenesis.

When you exercise, your brain experiences increases in cell volume, quantity and quality of connections between cells, and capillaries that deliver the vital glucose and oxygen required to keep the brain running. Considering the fact that we lose about 5-7% of brain volume each decade, the gains from exercise become critical just to maintain our current functioning. Fortunately, it doesn't take decades to see the benefit of exercise on brain structure.

In 2007, German researchers found that people learn vocabulary words 20 percent faster following exercise than they did before exercise, and that the rate of learning correlated directly with levels of BDNF (aka miracle grow).[5] Cell growth in the frontal and temporal lobes was seen after only 6 months of exercising just 3 times a week. In the scans, the exercisers' brains looked as if they were two to three years younger than they were. The researchers were unable to determine exactly what caused the growth, but they suggest multiple factors could play a role. "It could be new vascular structure, new neurons, new neuronal connections," Tucker, one of the lead researchers, says. "I think it's probably all of the above."[6]

Exercise improves learning by increasing alertness, attention, and motivation and by enhancing the physical structure of the brain through the development of new cells, and stronger connections between them.

Another potentially groundbreaking result of exercise is a decreased risk of developing Alzheimer's disease. Think of plaques or tangles in the brain associated with Alzheimer's as similar to running into an obstacle or detour. The tangles make it harder for one brain cell to communicate with the next. In addition to the brain-building effects discussed above, exercise also builds more pathways that may be able to bypass the tangles, providing more options when it comes to getting a message across.

With an increased number of connections in the brain, it makes sense that it would take longer to lose them as we age. Compare someone who has exercised for years to a couch potato. Who will lose muscle mass the fastest? The couch potato – because he had much less to begin with. Similarly, with more brain cells and more connections, it will take longer to lose them.

Use It or Lose It

As we age we lose muscle mass at the rate of approximately 5-7 pounds per decade, or about a half of a pound each year, unless we are actively training our body. The problem with muscle loss is not just that we lose strength, but that our metabolism slows down, causing us to store excess body fat. It is estimated that people add about 10 pounds of body weight each decade, which most people assume means they're gaining 10 pounds of fat. In fact, it's even worse than it seems.

Because our metabolism is slowing down, we are going to lose muscle as we age. So if we have a 10-pound shift in our body weight, but have lost muscle (due to a lack of strength training), we would have to add more than 10 pounds of fat to get the 10-pound gain. What looks like an increase of 10 pounds of fat is actually 15. This may not sound like much of a discrepancy, but calculate it out over several decades and watch what happens to your body fat percentage.

A 150-pound woman in her forties who gains about 10 pounds each decade will end up at about 190 pounds in her eighties. More problematic is the increase in her body fat percentage. At 150 pounds, she has 100 pounds of lean tissue (muscle, bones, water, organs, etc.) and 50 pounds of fat – a body fat percentage of just over 30%, which would put her in the moderately fat category. After the 40-pound weight gain, she has actually added 60 pounds of fat and her body fat percentage is now almost 60%, which puts her well into the obese category.

> *Note:* Body fat is calculated by taking the fat weight in pounds divided by the total weight in pounds. So 50 pounds of fat divided by 150 pounds is 33.3%. With the age-related weight gain, assuming muscle loss associated with a sedentary lifestyle, the new body fat percentage is the fat weight of 110 pounds divided by the new total weight of 190 pounds: 58%.

As we discussed in the previous chapter, this concept is important to keep in mind because body fat is associated with brain health and functioning in several ways. Excess body fat has a direct correlation to elevations of fat in the blood stream, and it increases the risk of diabetes. Both put strain on arteries, hindering the circulation of glucose and oxygen to the brain. Excess fat may also decrease sensitivity to insulin, which leads to excess sugar in the blood and can be toxic to the brain.

Keep in mind what we discussed about healthy weight in the Food is Fuel chapter: An obese person's brain will be significantly smaller in size than that of someone at a healthy weight.

Although most of the current research is being done on the impact of aerobic exercise and brain health because of its immediate brain boosting effects, it is important that we don't neglect the importance of strength training to keep our system functioning well over time.

Cognitive Fitness Benefits

Exercise has been shown to increase cognitive functions such as memory, learning, and overall quality of life. A study at the University of California, San Francisco showed that women who were more active showed less cognitive decline than those who were sedentary.[7] Not only did the group who walked about 17 miles a week (or about 45 minutes of walking, five days a week) maintain better cognitive functioning, researchers also found that every extra mile walked per week seemed to decrease the risk of cognitive decline by 13%, proving that every step counts.

According to Dr. Medina, a little bit of exercise goes a long way. Studies show that participating in some form of exercise just twice a week will give you benefits. "Bump it up to a 20-minute walk each day," he says, "and you will cut your risk of having a stroke – one of the leading causes of mental disability in the elderly – by 57%."[1]

Exercise is Medicine

Exercise also impacts the brain indirectly because it reduces risk of other diseases. While it initially puts stress on the system, exercise ends up enhancing immune functioning because the small amount of stress stimulates the body to break down just a little bit and then build back up stronger than before. Several studies show that employees who exercise regularly take fewer sick days and spend less money on health claims.

One company found that those who participated in their corporate exercise program took 80 percent fewer sick days. Another study showed that medical claims by employees who were members of a fitness center went down 27 percent, while nonmembers' claims rose by 17 percent. And according to a report published in the late 1990s, health-care claims at a major beverage corporation averaged $500 less for employees who joined the company's fitness program, compared with those who didn't.[5]

Heart disease is one of the largest killers in our world today. Exercise has been shown to increase healthy cholesterol in the blood stream that helps to eliminate unhealthy cholesterol. Just 30 minutes three times a week has been shown to decrease blood pressure and increase the ability of the heart and lungs to optimize circulation. By utilizing sugar in the blood and increasing insulin sensitivity, exercise keeps triglyercides from clouding arteries and decreases the risk of developing diabetes.

Projections suggest that by the year 2020, 1 out of 2 people will have diabetes, which we know has a direct impact on brain health and functioning. It is believed that the risk of developing type 2 diabetes – the most common form of the disease, which results from a decrease in insulin efficiency – may be cut in half with just a 5–10% decrease in body fat.[8]

Or Is It Better Than Medicine?

When it comes to mental health, exercise may prove to be even more beneficial than medication. *Spark* author John Ratey states that due to the ability of exercise to balance out chemicals in the brain, "going for a run is like taking a little bit of Prozac and a little bit of Ritalin because, like the drugs, exercise elevates these neurotransmitters."[5]

Because of its impact on brain chemicals involved with mood regulation, aerobic exercise has been shown to help alleviate depression and anxiety. Although it is not commonly discussed, depression is one of the nation's biggest health issues today. Depression currently effects approximately 15 million Americans a year. About 80% of people with depression are not currently seeking treatment of any kind, even though it is one of the most treatable illnesses with approximately 80-90% of people finding relief.[9]

When we exercise we reduce the tension in our muscles, which can decrease our perception of stress. Brain chemicals such as serotonin, dopamine, and gamma-aminobutyric acid (GABA) help calm mental activity, reduce stress, and increase feelings of happiness.[5] In a study at Duke University, when individuals with major depression were randomly assigned to a supervised or home exercise program, an antidepressant, or a combination of the two, exercisers were just as likely to enter into remission as those taking medication.[10] In fact, six months later relapse rates were lower with the exercise group, quite possibly because they were able to control the depression on their own, boosting their sense of self-efficacy.

Specific Recommendations

In order to have optimal circulation throughout the day, aim to get up and move your body at least every 90 minutes. If you have meetings that last longer than 90 minutes (which I'm sure you do), be sure to schedule stretch breaks. While you may have to sacrifice a few minutes of work, the return in energy will enable you to accomplish more in a shorter amount of time. When it comes to exercise, I suggest following the recommendations for optimal fitness in order to maximize your brainpower.

According to the American College of Sports Medicine (ACSM), individuals should aim to do moderate aerobic exercise for at least 30 minutes five days a week, or vigorous intensity exercise for at least 20 minutes three days a week.[11] Strength or resistance training should be performed at least two days a week. Do 2–3 sets with 8–12 reps per set, working out all of the major muscle groups (legs, chest, back, biceps, triceps, shoulders, abdominals, and back). Stretching should be done everyday, if possible, ideally after exercise when the muscles are warm.

You don't have to be an elite athlete to reap the numerous rewards of an exercise routine. Just 20 minutes of exercise five days a week is enough to not only promote good health, but also to see cardiovascular improvements, strength gains, and fat loss.[11] When it comes to strategic exercise, intensity is key. Most people focus on the hours they spend at the gym or the number of reps or sets they do. And they wonder why they're not seeing the results they expect from such a significant time investment.

However, look around and you'll notice that most people don't push themselves hard enough to really challenge their body. Again, it's not that you have to be grunting or doing deadlifts, but you certainly shouldn't feel comfortable. A 2002 study by the American Medical Association showed that a reduction in heart disease risk was linked to the intensity of exercise, not the amount of time spent working out.[12]

One of the best ways to make exercise something you can stick with over time is to play sports. In animal studies, forced exercise did not have the cognitive benefits of voluntary exercise, so pushing yourself to be miserable in the gym won't likely give you much of an advantage. This may be due to the fact that the negative impact of stress hormones cancels out the benefits from exercise.

Decrease "Activation Energy"

One of the challenges with exercise is that it often takes a lot of energy just to get started. This dilemma is especially problematic when we're feeling lethargic to begin with. Yet, you've probably had the experience of pushing yourself to go for a walk or hit the gym and within a few minutes you feel much more energized. One way to make physical activity a regular part of your life is to decrease what's called activation energy.

In physics, activation energy is the stimulus that's required to cause some sort of reaction. With human behavior, it's the energy we must first expend in order to do something. In his book, *The Happiness Advantage*, my friend Shawn Achor talks about his experience with activation energy when he was trying to practice guitar more frequently.[13] In his description of what he calls the 20-Second Rule, Shawn put the guitar closer to the couch and moved the remote further away – about 20 seconds away to be exact. "What I had done here, essentially, was put the desired behavior on the path of least resistance, so it actually took less energy for me to pick up and practice the guitar than to avoid it." He calls it the 20-second Rule "because lowering the barrier to change by just 20 seconds was all it took to help me form a new life habit."

Shawn recently told me about a strategy he used to help create a more consistent exercise routine. "I moved my athletic shoes right next to my bed and slept in my gym clothes for 21 days, decreasing the activation energy to exercise in the morning long enough to create a life habit." He also mentioned that he was very clear as to what type of exercise he was going to do each day, and he had a specific plan for that day's workout routine. When you don't plan ahead, you give your brain time to come up with a million excuses as to why it's better not to exercise. With all that time to contemplate, it's easy to talk your way out of it.

When it comes to increasing exercise consistency, and making healthier choices, Shawn has a few suggestions for applying the 20-Second Rule:

1. Keep your home exercise equipment on the first floor of your house or in a conspicuous place, where you will be more likely to use it, instead of in a dark bonus room in your house, where it is often used as storage space or a hanger for laundry. (Shawn also mentioned that a woman once told him that this strategy didn't work for her, so she was going to sleep on the treadmill.)

2. Put dumbbells next to the couch in your living room so that you don't have to go find them if you want to exercise while watching TV.

3. Pack a gym bag and take it with you to work so you have what you need to exercise during a break, or before you head home.

4. Put unhealthy food high up in your house so you have to get a step stool to get it. Food at eye level is easier to grab, so put your healthier options there.

Simply put, the goal is to make it easier to make healthy choices so that your brain will be less likely to talk you out of it!

Summary:
1. Look for opportunities to add movement to your day
2. Never sit for longer than 90 minutes at a time
3. Exercise aerobically at least 3x a week
4. Perform strength training exercises at least 2x a week
5. Decrease activation energy

"The handle on your recliner does not count as an exercise machine."

RULE #3
Balancing Stress Balances Life
"Our greatest weapon against stress is our ability to chose one thought over another." - William James

When we talk about stress management, many people assume that the goal should be to eliminate sources of stress. However, stress is not the enemy. In fact, life without stress would be a life without growth. It is often shocking to people to hear that one of the highest spikes in human mortality comes within about six months of retirement. Most people work hard their whole life, looking forward to the time when they can relax and enjoy the fruits of their labors. But our system is not designed to function in a state of all-or-nothing.

Stress can be defined in many different ways. At its most basic, stress is anything that causes something else to change. Obviously, this can be something negative, but it can also be something positive. When it comes to our body and brain, stress is anything that throws us out of balance (also known as allostatic load). When we are off balance, we will facilitate processes in our system to try to compensate. These can be seen in the body as a shift in metabolic functioning in areas such as our immune system, glucose regulation, and hormone production – with some hormones getting turned on and others turned off.

Change is a necessary part of life, and therefore our body and brain are well equipped to handle a significant amount of stress. The problem occurs when our stress gets too great in volume, or too intense in nature, and our system becomes overwhelmed.

Your brain is built to deal with stress that lasts about 30 seconds. Based on how your brain perceives stress, your body will produce different hormones designed to help stimulate your fight, flight, or freeze response. Stress that is immediate (or acute) only lasts for a short period of time, but chronic stress stimulates hormones like cortisol that are not quickly flushed through our system and can cause long-term damage.

Cortisol is so toxic to the brain that it can kill brain cells on contact.[1] According to stress researcher Robert Sapolsky, "for the vast majority of beasts on this planet, stress is about a short-term crisis, after which it's either over with or you're over with."[2] But for us humans, stress can last for days, months, or years at a time, giving cortisol hormones plenty of time to linger in our system, causing major damage.

When stress levels become too much for the brain to handle, damage can be seen to virtually every kind of cognition: memory and executive function, motor skills, immune response, sleep, and mental/emotional health. With an emergency on hand, it makes sense that the processes in the body considered long-term building projects (such as sleep, immune functioning, muscle repair, etc.) are put on hold while the immediate needs are taken care of (increased blood flow to get glucose and oxygen to the cells to take care of business).

Researchers have long studied elite performers in sports to determine how the brain works during times of peak performance. A recent article in *Golf Digest* discussed a study evaluating the brain activity of rookies vs. longtime pros. The more stressed amateur golfers showed higher activity levels in the areas of the brain that control our survival-based functioning (the limbic system); the pros didn't have as much activity in that area. This highlights the difference between a "clutch" brain and a stressed brain. A "clutch" brain is one that performs under pressure, and gains in this area is one of the many benefits of flexibility training and resilience strategies like relaxation techniques.[3]

I recently had an opportunity to speak with golf legend Sir Nick Faldo, and I asked him what he did to achieve a "clutch brain" when it mattered most. Nick told me that he used "verbal commands" to focus on what he wanted to do, and then how he was going to do it. Rather than being distracted with negative thoughts, he stayed focused on the positive, which seems like an easy thing to do unless you play golf and have tried to avoid paying attention to the bunkers, water hazards, and a recent case of the "yips." Nick also utilized visualization, which we will talk about more in the strength training section, to see himself hitting just the right shot.

What I appreciated most in our conversation was when Nick mentioned that there are several different ways to get in the right mind-set for golf, and that it's important for people to find out what works for them individually. "One of the problems with mental coaching is that many people think they have the one right solution for what everyone should do," he said. "There is no right or wrong way; you just have to find what works for you, and that will be the correct way." More focusing techniques will be discussed in Part Two so you can explore ways that will work best for you.

The Cortisol Connection

One of the primary culprits in stress-related damage to the body and the brain is the stress hormone cortisol. Many of you are likely familiar with cortisol from late-night infomercials touting supplements that supposedly block or decrease the impact of cortisol, helping to prevent mid-section weight gain. But if you spent money on these pills, you quickly learned that they don't work.

Cortisol is a steroid hormone released by the adrenal gland in response to stress. Compared with other fight-or-flight hormones like adrenaline, cortisol has a more lasting impact on the body. It remains in the blood stream for a longer period of time and causes unique shifts to occur in energy metabolism. Key functions of cortisol include increasing available blood sugar (breakdown of glucose from storage in fat and muscle), decreasing insulin efficiency (to keep blood sugar high), and suppressing immune functioning. While these effects are important to fuel the body in stressful situations, chronic exposure to cortisol has been shown to increase risk of diseases such as atherosclerosis and diabetes, and could potentially be linked to Alzheimer's and dementia.

Cortisol is an important player in the survival game for humans and other animals. The main purpose of cortisol is to stimulate a stress response that prepares the body and brain for continued threats to the system, and prepares them for threats in the future. Cortisol acts as a stimulant to the brain to increase consumption of food, particularly carbohydrates and fat. It also signals fat cells to retain as much energy as possible in fat stores, even in the midst of calorie deprivation. Cortisol slows metabolism—to keep energy demands to a minimum—by blocking many important metabolic hormones, including insulin, serotonin, growth hormone, testosterone, and estrogen.

Chronic stress can lead to an overabundance of cortisol, which can wreak havoc on our system in the short and long term. Researchers at the University of Colorado found that athletes who were overtraining had higher levels of cortisol, more frequent mood disturbances, suppressed immune functioning, and increased levels of body fat versus athletes who were not overtrained.[4] Among the athletes monitored, those who put in the most amount of training (runners with the most mileage and longest training hours) had the highest levels of cortisol, highest body fat, and highest scores on measures of depression. Researchers at Yale and the University of California, San Francisco found that among women in their study, cortisol had a direct correlation with both appetite and mood. The higher the cortisol level, the more the women ate sweets and experienced a negative mood.[5]

All of the elements of the *SYNERGY Fab 5* (nutrition, activity, relaxation, sleep, and social connections) play a role in successfully managing cortisol levels.

Stress and Memory

It is interesting to note that acute stress (do something about it right now) actually improves memory. We need to remember how we escaped the last time we were in a bind like this. Long-term stress, however, causes the body and brain to break down.

Dr. Sapolsky gives an excellent explanation in his book, *Why Zebras Don't Get Ulcers,* that I think is worth repeating. Fighting off threats requires our best resources – it's like having our elite military team fired up and ready to protect us. However, this comes at a cost. Keeping all of our best fighters on high alert requires a lot of energy, so at some point when it seems that the stress is going to be around for a while, those resources are pulled away for other functions and we end up with a compromised protection system.[2]

This is similar to what happens with our immune system – designed to protect us from harm, after a while it just runs out of gas and we are compromised and much more likely to develop illness, injury, and disease. What's more, when we run down our protectors, they become more likely to turn against their own troops (which happens in the body when the immune system starts to attack healthy cells, as in autoimmune disorders).

Recovery Is Not an Option

One of the most challenging things for busy professionals to do is to add recovery strategies to their routine. For some reason it's much easier for us to do something than not do anything. Blame it on the busyness of our world, constant access to technology, or the need to be connected 24/7. It's really uncomfortable to just be still. But like other healthy habits we want to form, relaxation is something that needs to be practiced in order to become more routine. Meditation, music, massage, hobbies, walking outside... the key is figuring out what works for you.

The "Vacation Diet"

A couple of years ago, while working on my dissertation (on the impact of stress on weight management, which ironically "caused" me to gain 10 pounds), I decided to try an experiment I called "The Vacation Diet." I put together a plan that included scheduling, accountability, and four key strategies: never letting myself get too hungry, staying active, having fun, and being relaxed. That was it. I put no limitations on what I ate or how much I ate. I was at a golf tournament, after all. (Fortunately, I play much too poorly to let it stress me out.) I even allowed myself a drink or two in the evenings if I wanted them at the social functions. I ate burgers and fries (that I shared with my golf partner), cookies (that I "shared" with a bird that scooped the second half out of my golf cart), and drank beer and wine.

But it was more than just looking at the calories in and calories out, in this case. I wanted to test the impact of creating more balance, getting recovery and relaxation, and truly enjoying food and drink in moderation while getting regular activity and exercise. (That's pretty much everything I think a good diet should consist of.)

To stick with my plan, I needed a strategy, which included relaxing, setting boundaries with regards to my time and energy, and striving for moderation. I forced myself, as difficult as it was, to set limits for time spent on the computer and blocked specific time slots for checking email, which was limited to once a day for the first few days and then not at all for the last few. There was nothing magical about this plan, but it worked because I was committed to following my own rules.

Although I couldn't stay on vacation the rest of my life (bummer), I decided on my "reality plan" to commit to continuing to set healthy boundaries for myself, checking emails only two or three times daily, depending on my priorities, in order to limit multitasking (still working on this one).

While you may feel like you have no time to schedule recovery, decreasing multitasking just might give you precious time back that you could invest in taking care of yourself. Numerous studies show that precious time and energy is lost shifting between tasks. Considering how much time we waste multitasking, if we work on our mental strength training we can end up with plenty of time to go to the gym or get a massage, even when we feel like there just isn't time to spend.

Oscillation Is Optimal

In his book *Corporate Athlete,* one of my mentors Jack Groppel discusses the need for humans to oscillate throughout the day. Dr. Groppel states, "an ideal daily energy curve ensures a proper balance between the discharge and recharge of energy: This can be calculated by the alternation between stages of effort and recovery."[6] Instead of living our life like one long marathon, he suggests we aim to live life in a series of sprints, alternating between periods of full engagement and strategic disengagement. This allows us to get enough stress to simulate growth without overloading the system. "The solution is simple," he says. "Make waves! Think about the reassuring 'beep' of an electrocardiogram and its waves. A sign of life!" I suggest that you break down each day (and within each day, each hour) into a series of sprints so that you can maximize your mental focus.

Chunking is a great strategy for enhancing our focus, so that we can actually get more done in less time. There are several different ways to use this technique of breaking down periods of time, activities, or goals into smaller, more manageable pieces. One easy way to create more oscillation is to use time blocks during which you dedicate specific periods of time to specific tasks.

You can maximize the effectiveness of time blocking by scheduling similar tasks in consecutive blocks. For example, separate your administrative tasks and plan to do only those items during the first hour or two in the morning, before you start to tackle email (which can quickly change your train of thought or cause you to multitask). If you have to manage financial issues such as paying bills or scheduling invoices, try to do all of them within the same time block. This allows your brain to focus on a particular aspect of your business (or your home life), which reduces brain strain by keeping you from jumping between different types of mental abilities.

Make sure that in between your time blocks you schedule adequate time for breaks. I recommend using 50-minute blocks so that you have 10 minutes each hour to do something that allows you to take a mental time out. You can maximize your cognitive benefits by adding something fun, engaging a social connection, or doing some physical activity during that time. In order to make sure the hours don't start blending into one big chunk, find some way to alert yourself when it's time to stop for a few minutes. You can set an alarm on your watch, phone, or computer – or ask someone else to meet up with you at a specific time to help boost accountability.

Many recent studies show that this type of oscillation throughout the day has immediate performance benefits. Taking breaks not only gives the brain a chance to rest, it increases focus and attention when we come back to a task. No doubt you've experienced frustration after working on a problem for an extended period of time, and after taking a break, you returned to find the answer right in front of your eyes.

Sometimes the best way to see a solution is to step away from it for a while, shifting your mental energy to something else (either a different task, or even better, a mental break). This allows us to break up mental monotony, which can cause our brain to go on automatic pilot. That's when we tend to become more rigid and less able to see new possibilities.

"Constant stimulation is registered by our brains as unimportant, to the point that the brains erases it from our awareness," according to Alejandro Lleras at the University of Illinois, who led a recent study validating the importance of mental breaks to maintain focus.[7]

Taking It Easy Is Hard

Just like anything that's not practiced regularly, relaxation can be quite challenging. We are so used to rushing around at a busy pace that many of us have developed "stress addiction," and experience major withdrawal when we try to slow down. Studies on stress show that even negative situations can cause a rush of positive endorphins in the brain. Why? Endorphins are designed to help us cope with an emergency by stimulating some of the same areas involved with rewarding us for positive behavior.

Dopamine, for example, is released when we have the expectation of something positive, such as in a phone call or email. However, once we say hello or open the email message we may find that what is waiting for us is actually something stressful. At this point the dopamine has been released, and brain connections are becoming stimulated. Lose this "rush," and you can find yourself feeling sluggish and unmotivated.

If you feel addicted to stress, you just might be. This doesn't mean that you're doomed for gloom. It just means that relaxation and recovery are going to take even more effort and careful planning to incorporate into your routine. Practice relaxation techniques regularly, manage energy consistently throughout the day, and you'll find yourself less and less dependent on the stress rush to keep you going.

Self-Care Must Be Scheduled

We hear it all the time. In order to be helpful to those around us, we must first take care of ourselves. Or as the pre-flight message consistently states, "please put on your oxygen mask first before assisting others." This isn't just for your benefit – if you run out of fuel, you can't be helpful to anyone else. Case closed. In my work with professionals, both in sport and in business, it's pretty much the same. The message regarding the importance of self-care is constantly communicated but seldom fully grasped.

People pour their blood, sweat, and tears into a career that often uses up all of their energy, and yet confess that they "do it all for their family." But ask their family what they want most from this person, and the answer almost always has the same tune – they want more of the person's energy and engagement when he or she is around. To pour everything you have into providing for others, but not be able to be fully present when you're with them, can leave people feeling neglected, despite all of your efforts.

What people want most from us is our energy and engagement, and in order to be fully present with them, it is critical that we replenish our energy on a regular basis. Scheduling time to take care of ourselves is not something that can get pushed aside – not if we want to be our best self for the people and things that matter most. We need to put recharge appointments in our calendar to make sure we refill our own energy tank, or we will continue to run on fumes, just getting by and never being fully engaged or completely present. Schedule time for yourself, and you are investing in everything else that is important to you. We all know this – we just need to act like we believe it.

(For more information about the impact of stress on the brain, see *Why Zebras Don't Have Ulcers* by Robert Zapolsky.)

Summary:
1. Stress is necessary
2. Recovery is not an option
3. Oscillating is optimal
4. Practice makes relaxation easier
5. Self care must be scheduled

Copyright 2006 by Randy Glasbergen. www.glasbergen.com

"I'm finally learning how to relax.
Unfortunately, relaxation makes me tense."

RULE #4
Resting Is Working

"Sleep is not a vast wasteland of inactivity. The sleeping brain is highly active at various times during the night, performing numerous physiological, neurological and biochemical housekeeping tasks." – Dr James B. Maas

According to the National Sleep Foundation, approximately 70 million Americans are affected by chronic sleep loss or sleep disorders. The annual costs associated with chronic sleep loss are estimated at $16 billion in health care expenses and $150 billion in lost productivity.[1]

Sleep deprivation and sleepiness have adverse effects on performance, response times, accuracy, attention, and concentration. Lack of quality sleep has been associated with a wide range of quality-of-life measures, such as social functioning, mental and physical health, and even early death.[2]

In one of my workshops I spoke with a physician who was struggling with sleep deprivation. He told me that he had recently been pulled over by the police twice in one evening, on suspicion of driving under the influence. In this case, he was driving sleepy. Considering the fact that people who are suffering from lack of sleep perform just as poorly as people who are drunk in driving simulation tests, maybe we should start penalizing those who are sleepy at the wheel.

Sleep is Critical to Repair and Rebuild
Sleep is not just about giving our system a rest. In fact, it's during sleep that our body and brain do some of their most important work repairing and rebuilding muscle tissue and creating stronger neural connections in the brain that improve learning and memory. The area of the brain that may be most affected by sleep, or the lack of it, is the prefrontal cortex –

responsible for your "executive functioning" processes such as learning, judgment, reasoning, memory consolidation, and understanding.

In his book *Sleep for Success*, Dr. James Maas states that someone who is sleep-deprived is operating with about 50% less memory ability.[3] Maas says that the final two hours of sleep, from approximately hours 6–8, are crucial for memories to become fixed in the brain. It is during this time that most of us experience REM sleep, when the events of the day are replayed over and over again to become stored in our mental filing cabinet.

Studies with animals and humans suggest that brain activity occurring during the day is reactivated during sleep as your brain is consolidating memory. Just like the muscles in our body, the connections in our brain require rest to do the work of forming stronger pathways, repairing, and rebuilding.

A recent study published in *Nature Neuroscience* evaluated the impact of sleep on memory. According to researcher Jan Born, the activation of brain cells during slow-wave sleep not only strengthens our memory, it also supports the transfer of the memory from short-term storage in the hippocampus to long-term storage in the neocortex.[4]

I recently had a chance to speak with a friend of mine, Admiral Ray Smith, who served as a Navy Seal for 31 years, and commander of the Seals for four years. Not only does Admiral Smith have an amazing military background, but he also continues to compete in some of the most extreme adventure races around. I spoke with him about lessons he learned from his time in the Navy, as well as throughout his decades of athletic competition. One of the primary changes he made as he gained experience (and added years) was to his sleep routine. "I remember when I was young, I'd focus on maximizing the amount of time I spent working, training, or competing," he said. "As I have gotten older, I notice more and more the impact of sleep on my cognitive functioning, and I will not compromise sleep."

Sleepy Body, Sleepy Brain

Numerous studies show the impact of sleep deprivation on performance and health. According to the National Institutes of Health, sleeping less than 6 hours can have a serious effect on your ability to think and act properly, even if you feel as though you are functioning just fine.[5] In a study at the University of Pennsylvania, researchers found that subjects who slept 4–6 hours a night for 14 consecutive nights showed deficits in cognitive performance equivalent to how they would perform after going without sleep for up to three days in a row.[6]

Lack of sleep has been correlated with obesity, increases in smoking and alcohol use, inactivity, inflammation and heart disease, blood sugar imbalances, and increases in stress hormones such as adrenaline and cortisol.[7] A lack of sleep puts your body under additional stress, which may trigger the stress response: increasing adrenaline, cortisol, and other stress hormones during the day.

By missing out on adequate sleep, your body is not able to go through the proper recovery cycles, which means you also miss the opportunity for your blood pressure to dip during the evening. This may negatively impact your heart and vascular system by increasing CRP (C-Reactive Protein, released when there is inflammation in the body), which has been shown to increase the risk of developing heart disease. Immune functioning is compromised by too little sleep because we miss the opportunity to produce the necessary hormones and other molecules needed for fighting off infection.

Sleep is the body's natural recovery phase. If we eliminate the necessary balancing process achieved when we sleep well, our system becomes out of balance and we will experience symptoms in a variety of physical, emotional, and mental ways.

How Much is Enough?

The amount of sleep that is optimal for brain health and performance is unique to each individual. To determine how much sleep you need, you have to find out how much time it takes for you to wake up feeling refreshed, without needing an alarm clock. Studies show that humans need 6–10 hours of sleep each night, which is why you've most likely heard the recommendation for an average of 8 hours each night.

However, some people can function well with 6 hours of sleep while other people need the whole 10. According to recent research, dipping below the 6-hour mark impairs cognitive functioning for just about everyone, so it is recommended that you always get at least 6 hours of quality sleep each night.

How Do You Know If You're Not Getting Enough Sleep?

1. You're dependent on an alarm clock. If you're getting enough sleep, you should be able to wake up on time without a morning alarm.

2. You're driving drowsy. Falling asleep at the wheel is a sure sign that you are too tired. It's also dangerous – drowsy driving is a common cause of deadly auto accidents.

3. You're attached to the coffee pot. A cup of coffee to start your day is fine, but you shouldn't have to rely on coffee, or other energy drinks, to stay awake.

4. You're making mistakes. It's harder to focus and concentrate when you are tired. You're more easily distracted and less likely to catch and fix errors.

5. You're forgetful. Sleep loss may explain why you have a hard time remembering things. Sleep deprivation hinders short-term memory.

6. You're snippy and irritable. Being tired can have a negative effect on your moods. It makes you more likely to feel depressed, anxious, and frustrated.

7. You're frequently sick. Without sleep your immune system is not at full strength. It's harder for your body to fight illness.

Oscillation Improves Sleep

As we discussed in the section on stress management, oscillation is important. We need to pay attention to its benefits. Instead of seeing our day as one long marathon, breaking it up into smaller chunks allows us not only to be more focused, but also to get strategic breaks that will improve our ability to recover more effectively and efficiently. By incorporating relaxation strategies throughout the day, we bring stress levels down so we aren't trying to fall asleep after a constant rush of adrenaline. We can't go at light speed all day long and expect our system to come to a screeching halt once we crawl into bed.

It always catches me off guard when my clients seem surprised that they aren't sleeping well, or feel tired throughout the day. The first question I always ask: "Do you take breaks during the day?" While it may seem like this has nothing to do with sleep, in my opinion it is one of the most important factors. Even if you utilize healthy sleep rituals, limit caffeine, and turn off distractions, your brain can't immediately turn off just because you tell it to after you have been going at a hectic pace all day.

The Importance of Rituals

Have you ever tried to read a book before bed? If you're like most people, you only make it through a few pages and probably read the same section over and over again. There are several reasons why reading helps to induce sleep. It takes your mind off the worries or stress of the day, and it may provide relaxation through entertainment. But the driving force behind this phenomenon is the brain training that occurs as a result of repeatedly connecting a place (bed), an activity (reading), and a desired outcome (falling asleep).

We could derive similar results with other strategies that utilize the same principles – mind calming and relaxing. For example, if you regularly take a bath before bed and listen to music, you can practice focusing your mind on relaxation, and the cooling down process of getting out of the warm water will enhance sleep. Whether it's reading a book, taking a bath, drinking warm milk, going for a walk, lighting a favorite candle and listening to music, or any other mind calming, relaxing activity you can think of to do at bedtime, the more you associate that behavior with sleep, the more your brain will begin to anticipate the connection, and the quicker you will find yourself in restful slumber.

Sleep Strategies

Some activities are important to avoid before bedtime. Others can assist you in falling asleep and staying asleep long enough to feel rested. Here are a few tips for sleeping well:

- *Go to bed early.* Some studies suggest that early to bed and early to rise is more suited for our natural rhythms.
- *Get out of bed.* If you have trouble falling asleep, get out of bed and do something relaxing until you feel sleepy.
- *Limit naps.* If you take a nap, keep it brief. Nap for less than an hour and before 3 p.m.
- *Wake up on the weekend.* It is best to go to bed and wake up at the same times on the weekend as you do during the work week. This enables you to build a steady pattern around your sleep schedule.
- *Avoid late-day caffeine.* Avoid caffeine in the afternoon and at night. It stays in your system for hours and can make it hard for you to fall asleep.
- *Adjust the lights.* Dim the lights in the evening so your body knows it will soon be time to sleep. Let in the sunlight in the morning to boost your alertness.
- *Wind down.* Take some time to "wind down" before going to bed. Get away from the computer, turn off the TV and your cell phone, and relax quietly for 15 – 30 minutes. Parents should keep TVs and computers out of their children's bedrooms.
- *Eat a little.* Never eat a large meal right before bedtime. While a big meal may cause you to feel drowsy, your body will have to work hard to process all of that food, which can actually be stimulating to your system. Enjoy a healthy snack or light dessert so you don't go to bed hungry.
- *Avoid alcohol.* A drink or two may help you fall asleep, but it may also keep you from getting the quality of

sleep you need. Alcohol is quickly metabolized by the body and has a stimulating effect on the brain, disrupting sleep even when you don't wake up.

(For more information on sleep, including when you should see a sleep specialist, visit the National Sleep Foundation at www.nationalsleepfoundation.org.)

Summary:
1. We work while we sleep
2. Sleep is critical for repairing and rebuilding
3. Most people require 6–8 hours of sleep
4. Breaks during the day help facilitate healthy oscillation
5. Bedtime rituals induce optimal sleep

"I toss and turn all night and you won't count that as an eight-hour aerobic workout?!"

RULE #5
A Social Life is Life Support

"If you want to go fast, go alone.
If you want to go far, go together."

African proverb

Finally, we come to what might be the most critical indicator of long-term health: social connection. With all the technological advances we have to keep us connected across the globe, you might think we are more social than ever. However, this constant preoccupation with staying connected has actually torn apart the concept of relationships as we once knew it.

Keep in mind that social connection is based on how you feel, not necessarily on the number of friends you have or whether you're married or single. A recent study at Harvard examined data from more than 309,000 people and found that a lack of strong relationships increased the risk of premature death from all causes by 50% – an effect comparable to smoking up to 15 cigarettes a day, and greater than obesity and physical inactivity.[1] George Vaillant, director for 40 years of the Harvard project "The Study of Adult Development," states there are "70 years of evidence that our relationships with other people matter, and matter more than anything else in the world."[2]

Loneliness Is Bad for Your Health
When it comes to our survival instincts, being part of the right crowd may be one of the most important strategies to keeping us alive. Researchers often trigger the physiological stress response in animals by removing them from their social structure; simply isolating them activates stress hormones. The same is true in humans. Loneliness is a threat to survival.

In their book, *Loneliness: Human Nature and the Need for Social Connection*, John Cacioppo and William Patrick argue that loneliness, like hunger, is an alarm signal that evolved hundreds of thousands of years ago when group cohesion was essential to fight off attacks.[3] In a study with children, students were divided into groups and asked to evaluate bite-sized cookies. Before tasting the cookies, one group was told that no one wanted to work with them, while the other group was told that everyone wanted to work with them but that they'd still have to work on their own because it would be impossible to work with so many people. Each student was then handed a plate of cookies and told to evaluate them. In the group that was told everyone wanted to work with them, students ate an average of 4.5 cookies, but in the rejected group they ate 9. The authors asked, "Is it any wonder we turn to ice cream when we're sitting at home feeling all alone in the world?"[3]

As research continues to look at the relevance of social connections, a new field of social science has emerged. Social neuroscience looks at the associations between social and neural connections, and determines the impact of our relationships on health and well-being. Dr. Cacioppo and Dr. Gary Berntson have been credited with founding the social neuroscience movement. By evaluating brain scans and monitoring physiological responses, Cacioppo and Berntson found that there was an overpowering influence of social context, or a sense of connection, on the brain and the body. In fact, the impact was so intense that they were able to see changes to the genetic expression in white blood cells.

Cacioppo's research shows that loneliness can cause increases in blood pressure, stress, depression and anxiety, and cortisol production. Feeling lonely changes behavior, as well. Studies have connected loneliness with a decrease in exercise frequency, an increase in caloric consumption (specifically comfort foods high in processed carbohydrates), and an increase in alcohol and drug consumption (both prescription and illegal).[3]

Loneliness negatively affects immune functioning, impairs quality sleep, and has also been correlated to the risk of developing Alzheimer's disease. Unfortunately, loneliness can be a vicious cycle, in that it can trigger a sense of sadness that causes even more isolation and an even greater sense of loneliness.

According to positive-psychology experts Martin Seligman and Christopher Peterson, very little that is positive in life happens in isolation. Consider the last time you laughed so hard that you cried, or the last time you were overwhelmed with feelings of joy. How about the last time you felt incredibly proud of an accomplishment? Most likely, you weren't alone. Experts agree that relationships may be the most important contributor to overall life satisfaction and emotional well-being among people of all ages and cultures.[4]

Connection Is Based on Perception

Although relationships are incredibly enriching, being alone doesn't have to be lonely – which is a good thing, considering how many of us are in fact alone. The latest Census figures indicate there are some 31 million Americans living alone, which accounts for more than a quarter of all US households. There are many benefits to being on your own. Quality time in solitude can help us to unwind and recharge so that we have more energy to give to the people around us. Some studies also highlight the benefit of isolation for certain cognitive functions, such as memory (concentrating more when we think we're alone), empathy (taking time to think through how others may feel), focus (decreasing multitasking), and judgment (not being influenced by other's perspectives).

But just being surrounded by people doesn't guarantee a sense of connection or belonging. As Henry David Thoreau once said, "I never found the companion that was so companionable as solitude. We are for the most part more lonely when we go abroad among men than when we stay in our chambers." It is our personal perspective that carries the most weight when it comes to how our relationships influence our brain.

Like most things health-related, it seems that the key to making alone time beneficial is following the "all things in moderation" recommendation. Too much solitude is clearly damaging to our body and our mind, but too much busyness can also limit our opportunities to reflect, make connections, and experience personal insight.

Many people find it difficult to create time to disconnect. If you feel like you are too busy to take some quiet time to yourself, consider the following recommendations:

1. Turn off the television. Adults spend an average of 170 minutes a day watching TV and movies (which, by the way, is nine times the number of minutes spent on all leisure-time physical activities combined).[5] While this may feel like a nice mental vacation, it's not the best way to quiet your mind because you continue to receive stimulation, whether you are aware of it or not. It doesn't mean TV is off limits, but you may get some good "me time" by decreasing the amount you watch even by 30 minutes a day.

2. Decrease use of the internet. Many people think that Facebook and other social media outlets keep them connected, but it can often be at a superficial level. By disconnecting from the computer a bit more often, you can actually give yourself time to pause and reflect, or even get some one-on-one time with someone you care about. Try to limit email time to certain times during the day so it's not a constant distraction.

3. Wake up earlier. Try getting up just 30 minutes earlier to spend time reflecting on your day. Beginning with journaling or meditation can be a great way to get your mind focused on what's ahead, and writing down things you're grateful for can put you in an optimistic mind-set.

Keep in mind that how we feel is completely based on our perception of what's going on, not the specifics regarding how often we are social, whether we are single or married, or the number of friends we have. The negative consequences of loneliness most likely have more to do with the anxiety or depression that can result from feeling alone than the actual state of being by yourself.

While staying connected is definitely an important part of brain health, working on your perception can also decrease your sense of loneliness at times when you may not be as connected as you would like. You can learn specific strategies for creating a healthy perspective and mindset in the flexibility training section in Part Two.

Connection Boosts the Mind and Body

Feeling connected to other people can change us, both physically and mentally, for the better. In 2008, Ybarra and his colleagues evaluated the social engagement of 3,600 people aged 24 to 96 and found that the more connected people were, the better they performed on a mental exam.[6] When we make a positive social connection, our brain releases a feel-good chemical called oxytocin, which instantly reduces anxiety and improves focus and concentration.[7]

People who receive support during the healing process are shown to have improved chances of recovery. Heart attack survivors were 3 times more likely to survive when they received support[8], and participating in a breast cancer support group doubled life expectancy post-surgery[9]. The amount of stress we feel about something challenging is modified when we are with someone we care about. In a study of perception, participants who were accompanied by a friend estimated a hill to be less steep than those who were alone.[10]

Connection also increases our sense of purpose. When we feel connected to other people, there is a direct correlation with our sense of meaning in life. Just going through the motions and surviving another day doesn't seem to be enough when relationships are involved.

SHARP Science - In the Gallup well-being study, people who had a best friend at work (only 30% of Americans) were seven times more likely to be engaged with their job, exhibited higher sales and profitability, engaged customers better, produced higher quality work, had greater commitment to the firm's mission, had better safety records (since friends often made sure they were complying with safety precautions), were happier at work, and had a higher chance of sticking with a firm. Of the workers who didn't have a best friend, only 8% of them were engaged in their job.[11]

Quantity vs. Quality

The problem with being overly connected – as you may have realized if you're a "social networker" – is that it's impossible to maintain the same depth of connection with so many people. Take Facebook as an example. Many of my friends (all 364... wait... 365, and counting) brag about the number of connections they have (not me, of course, at least not until I have a more brag-worthy number). But ask them what is currently going on in the lives of each of their "friends," and they'll most likely look at you like your crazy (and then de-friend you).

Social networking websites and tools are great for expanding your quantity of connections, but you will quickly see that it is impossible to keep up with what every single friend is doing. With hundreds of new posts every day it would require a full time commitment to stay on top of it. That said, I still use Facebook and find it very valuable when I'm conducting a survey, trying to find a good restaurant in a town I'm visiting, or looking to vent about my travel schedule (thanks FB friends for listening). But when it comes to feeling connected, or avoiding loneliness, social networking sites just don't seem to cut it for most people.

What really matters is the quality of our relationships, much more than the quantity. In fact, someone may have few friends but still feel fully engaged socially. While marriage was once thought to help people feel connected, it turns out that it's the quality of the relationship (no surprise here), not marital status, that determines the potential benefit (which, as a single person, made me feel much better).

Building Better Relationships

One of the best ways to strengthen existing relationships is to dedicate focused time to people we care about. My clients often complain about not having enough time to spend with the people they love. I like to remind them that it's not necessarily about the time we are able to share, but the quality of the energy we bring to the time we have.

As busy professionals, we all know how challenging it can be to get home at a decent hour. For most of my clients, being there in time to have meals with family usually means speeding through traffic lights, taking calls on a cell phone while driving, and rushing in the door still fully focused on issues at work.

Often in our attempt to spend "quality time" with the people who matter most to us, we forget that it's our full attention that people want most. After all, who is the guy (or gal) who walks in the door still stressed about work yet patting himself on the back for "being there" for his family? Probably the same guy who paces the sidelines of his child's sporting event while typing away on his smartphone or checking email. Probably the same guy who drills the family with questions about what they accomplished during the day, is critical with his feedback, eats as quickly as he raced home, and then passes out on the couch in a "food coma." Is this really *being there* for your family?

We've all experienced times when we've been physically present and completely absent mentally or emotionally. We've also all had occasions when we didn't have much time available but managed to have an extraordinary experience because we were fully focused in the moment.

When it comes to our relationships, there is nothing that people want more from us than our attention, right here, right now. Practicing focusing exercises, such as those described in the next section, will help you train yourself to be more present for the people and things that matter most to you.

Social "Cross Training"

To increase your sense of connection, take a look at your current schedule and try to identify times that you could either reach out to someone for a conversation or ask someone to join you on a task or activity. This is a great opportunity for mental "cross training." Grab a friend or colleague to go for a walk so you can exercise while you connect. Or ask a family member to join you for a movie so you can improve your connection with them while getting some relaxation (if you chose the right movie, and the right family member, of course).

Summary:

1. Isolation can be bad for your health
2. Social connection is based on perception
3. Being alone doesn't have to be lonely
4. Schedule social engagements
5. Cross train with social activities that boost health

© Randy Glasbergen
www.glasbergen.com

"If a tree falls in the forest, but you don't hear about it on Facebook, MySpace, YouTube or Twitter, did it really happen?"

PART TWO – TRAIN COGNITIVE FITNESS

Introduction to Cognitive Fitness

Cognitive fitness is the ability of the brain to focus your mental energy on the things that matter most to you, in order to maximize your health, happiness, and performance. Just like physical fitness, mental fitness requires several complementary elements of training to optimize strength, flexibility, and endurance.

In the sections that follow, we will discuss each of these dimensions of fitness in more detail, including why each is important and how specifically we can train to improve our abilities. Each section will conclude with exercises that have real-world applications, with the top techniques for each training target, sprint workout options that only require 30 seconds to 2 minutes of training time, and the training takeaway that highlights the key point of that section. *SHARP Science* notes will also be included, providing a scientific reference for those who are interested in the data.

STEP FOUR
Build Mental Muscle (strength training)

Resistance Training – Building Mental Muscle

A strong brain allows you to focus your mental energy in a way that helps maximize your performance. Our natural tendency to multitask often overrides our need to focus on one thing at a time. A strong brain is able to fully engage the power of our mind, rather than getting distracted by everything else that's going on around us. The result: You optimize your productivity, efficiency, and overall performance.

Information Overload

With so many ways to stay connected these days, it's easy to find yourself feeling overloaded with information. What's interesting is that the younger you are, the less likely you even realize that you are constantly being bombarded with information and mental stimulus. Back in my day (never thought I'd hear myself say that), we had to get up and change the channel on the TV every time we wanted to watch a new program (or act as the channel changer for our parents or older siblings). In my day, the only people with cell phones or pagers were doctors or drug dealers. And if you wanted to read a book or use the computer, you went to the library.

Nowadays, we have a 24/7 connection to anything we want via a multitude of mini-computers on our smartphones, iPads, and laptop computers – even while flying in the friendly skies. It's also not uncommon to see elementary school kids carrying around their own cell phones, iPads, and laptops. In fact, my 6-year-old nephew and 4-year-old niece both seem to intuitively know how to use the same iPad that is still causing me frustration to learn (after 2 years of trying).

But while all this technology makes life easier, it also creates a big problem: We quickly become addicted to the constant "noise" and hardly recognize what's going on around us half the time. I had an opportunity to go to a remote spa retreat with a good friend a few months ago, and it was the first time I was truly not able to stay connected. Cell phone reception was completely impossible, and the wireless internet connection they promised us was erratic, at best. It was great!

On the third and final day, my friend said, "Hey, I think you just got here." We both laughed, knowing how difficult it is to slow down when we're used to running at such a crazy, chaotic pace. How long does it take you to feel like you're on vacation when you've taken some time off? Two, three days? All week? It seems to me that when we finally turn work off, we start worrying about all the work we'll be coming back to when we return. We convince ourselves that staying plugged in is better than having to try to catch up after the fact, so we never truly shut down.

When I returned to the real world, I was shocked at how loud everything was. I could barely stand to have the TV on. Everything I saw seemed to make me feel depressed or anxious. Sitting in a restaurant trying to write, I could barely hear myself think with the loud music blaring over the speakers. Unless we've taken time to be quiet for a while, when we're in the middle of the noise we usually don't even notice.

Although we may not realize it, constant environmental stimulus has a big impact on our mental energy. In fact, having to constantly try to tune out the world around us trains our brain to dismiss things that might actually be important.

In a recent article on information overload, Derek Dean and Caroline Webb of McKinsey & Company compared too much mental stimulation to eating too much food.[1] Many people eat more than they need as a way to distract themselves from their problems, or from tasks they just don't feel like dealing with. Sometimes, an overabundance of information provides the same task distraction, which can keep people from paying attention to what most needs their attention. The authors suggest that this happens by flooding us "with a variety of questions and topics that frequently could be addressed by others," which can distract us from the unpleasant issues we most need to deal with.

The pull to be constantly on and constantly connected is a serious problem in the business world, as it quickly begins to wear away at our priceless human capital. We all know that we need to protect and strategically manage our most valuable resources such as time and money, but we often burn through our mental capital like it's nothing, assuming it will always be there. In my workshops, this issue is a frequent topic of discussion, and oftentimes debate. Employees complain that they have no choice but to stay attached to their technological leashes (cell phones, text messages, emails, instant messenger, etc). But the key issue here is the story we tell ourselves that keeps us feeling so attached.

Most people have convinced themselves that they must respond ASAP or something horrible is going to happen. I'm not sure that anyone has played that tape out all the way to see how the story ends. What will happen if we don't respond immediately? Other than a few of my clients who are physicians, life and work will go on for the majority of us.

My challenge to the business professionals I work with is to determine who sets those expectations in the first place. If you respond within 2-3 minutes to every single email, people will expect you to keep it up. But if you have an established pattern, or norm, that tells people they will hear back from you within 24 or even 48 hours, you might be surprised to find out that for the majority of emails this time frame is more than sufficient. According to Dean and Webb, if we don't do something to change our current working norms, we are "…at risk of moving toward an ever less thoughtful and creative professional reality."[1]

Stress Addiction

Most people have literally become addicted to stress – a huge challenge as we try to change our business norms and become more balanced, thoughtful, and creative. Each time we anticipate a possibility for something pleasant, a bit of dopamine is released in the brain. This seems like a good thing, considering that dopamine, along with several other neurotransmitters, makes us feel good. But this release of feel-good chemicals is also at the core of addiction. The reward center in our brain plays an important role in facilitating behavior that is beneficial for us. Our most basic needs for survival, such as food and sex, stimulate the pleasure center in the brain to support our continued drive to sustain life.

However, this drive can also be supported by the brain when it anticipates or predicts that something positive might happen. The phone rings, you feel the vibration of your iPhone signaling a text message, the email alert sounds… these all signal the possibility that there is good or exciting news on the other end. Immediately dopamine is released in the brain in anticipation. While this may not seem like a big deal, it's exactly how the addiction process happens. Food, drugs, alcohol, sex, gambling – they all stimulate the same reward center, even though we know that some of these things may not actually be good for us (at least not in excess).

As dopamine falls, we can feel down, which can cause us to reach out again for the substance or behavior that initially triggered the response. The big problem occurs when this cycle is repeated. With each surge of dopamine we require more to reach the same high. And soon we require that rush just to bring us back to feeling normal again, causing us to experience cravings.

Because stress triggers the reward or pleasure center in the brain, it is a highly addictive stimulant. Fortunately, how we perceive and manage stress can alter our response, allowing us to have stress in our life in a healthy, balanced way. To do this, we must train our brain to interpret stress in healthy ways, and to build in adequate recovery on a daily basis. We will cover this in more detail in the next section.

Multitasking and Our Monkey Brain

With so many demands on your mental energy, it's easy to find yourself pulled in multiple directions. Jumping from one project to another may seem like the only option for getting things done; however, the negative impact on attention and focus is significant. Although being "good at multitasking" is often part of our job description, we need to change the way we look at multiple priorities so that our mental energy can be laser-focused on those things that really require our attention. While this approach may appear to take more time, the fact that we are actually getting more done in the time we have ends up saving us precious time in the long run while also increasing our productivity and performance.

Truth is, our brain is wired in a way that only allows it to focus on one thing at a time. Take juggling, for example. It may appear that you're doing several tasks at once, but you can only focus on one ball at a time – the rest are just floating in the air. The time it takes to switch our attention back and forth between tasks causes us to be much less efficient.

In a recent study, participants who completed two simultaneous tasks took up to 30 percent longer and made twice as many errors as those who completed the same tasks in sequence.[2] When we switch tasks, we have to turn our attention away from one task and then determine or recall the rules for completing the next task. Time management experts believe that it can take approximately 20 minutes to fully recover from shifting attention, with the time increasing for more complex tasks.

Another problem with multitasking is that it forces us to respond quickly, without time to assess the situation, consider multiple options, and then mindfully make a decision. This situation forces us to use our "monkey brain" (in case you were reading with your "monkey brain" earlier, you can read more about this back in step two).

Multitaskers also show higher levels of stress hormones than their more single-minded counterparts. Researchers at Reuters found that two-thirds of respondents believed that information overload had decreased job satisfaction and damaged their personal relationships. One-third believed it had damaged their health.[3] The added stress of multitasking can increase the amount of stress hormones that can damage brain cells over time. People who are multitasking too much often experience various warning signs such as difficulty with short-term memory, difficulty concentrating, or gaps in attentiveness.

Staying focused on one task at a time also benefits our personal relationships. We are more able to pay full attention to the people we are with. For those things that require multitasking, we may be able to tone our multitasking muscles through practice, stress management, and a good self-care regimen that provides us with proper nutrition, physical activity, and adequate sleep.

"It doesn't mean you can't do several things at the same time," says Dr. Marcel Just, co-director of Carnegie Mellon University's Center for Cognitive Brain Imaging. "But we're kidding ourselves if we think we can do so without cost."[4]

Building Focus, Concentration and Attention

"The difference between passing time and spending time wisely depends on making smart choices about what to pay attention to." – Dan Siegel, Mindsight[5]

Just like the muscles in our body, we need a strategy to help us build better mental capacities, such as focus, concentration, and attention. Although many of us have trained ourselves to be "good multitaskers" and fall into this pattern due to automatic pilot, we can create a new way of doing things by utilizing the training strategies of cognitive fitness. In her book *Rapt*, Winifred Gallagher reminds us, "Most failures occur despite effort, not due to a lack of it."[6] It's not about working longer hours or trying harder; it's about bringing the best energy we have to the time we have. Mental focus and attention are crucial to making sure that happens.

An important consideration when it comes to our mental energy is the impact of constant stimulus on the brain. Because there are so many things competing for our attention at any particular time, it is the brain's job to determine what is important and what can be ignored. Imagine if you were paying attention to everything around you right now at one time – you'd have an attention debt for sure. Our ability to tune out the unnecessary is critical for our brain to maintain optimal functioning. The drop in our attention resources is what cognitive scientists call "vigilance decrement."

According to University of Illinois psychology instructor and researcher Alejandro Lleras, "For 40 or 50 years, most papers published on the vigilance decrement treated attention as a limited resource that would get used up over time, and I believe that to be wrong. You start performing poorly on a task because you've stopped paying attention to it. But you are always paying attention to something."[7] The author proposes "deactivating and reactivating your goals" by taking brief mental breaks as a way to stay focused throughout the day, utilizing strategies such as those we discussed in the section on oscillation in step two.

Biofeedback

One of the most scientifically validated tools for training the brain to bring awareness and focus to the present moment is a method called biofeedback. This process uses specific instruments to measure physiological changes such as brainwaves, heart rate, breathing, muscle activity, and skin temperature. Biofeedback monitors provide specific feedback to the user in order to help the person see how his or her thoughts, emotions, and behaviors impact their body. With the aid of the technology, the individual is able to change certain aspects of inner processing (what's going on in the mind) to help create desired physical outcomes, such as inducing the relaxation response. With practice, you can bring about these changes without using the instrument, just by using the power of your mind.

Many high-quality studies show that biofeedback can be an effective treatment for migraine and tension headaches, high blood pressure, anxiety, post-traumatic stress disorder, depression, and a host of other physical and psychological conditions. Biofeedback techniques help to gauge how the body is responding to relaxation strategies, which can help minimize the negative impacts of stress, enhance recovery, and induce sleep. A specific class of biofeedback called neurofeedback (or EEG biofeedback) has been used to effectively treat attention deficit hyperactivity disorder (ADHD), and may help manage symptoms of other brain disorders such as autism, brain injuries, and seizures.

As the popularity of biofeedback continues to grow, more executives, athletes, and other performers use this process to help them get in the zone of peak performance. Techniques that were once available only through a medical professional can now be easily accessed at home through portable devices such as those at www.heartmath.com. Although the technology is quite simple to use, it would be a good idea to work with a biofeedback practitioner to help you get your program started.

(For more information on biofeedback, visit
The Association for Applied Psychophysiology
and Biofeedback at www.aapb.org.)

Distraction Resistance
What you do *not* pay attention to is probably more important than what you *do* pay attention to. Distractions are all around us, and when we are functioning in survival mode, those distractions cause our brain to skip around as it tries to

figure out what is a threat and what is not. Although we have been surrounded by these distractions for so long that we may not consciously notice them, our mind will continue to be on alert to protect us, just in case anything needs fighting off or running away from. Even little things in our environment can cause brain jumping, moving from one thing to another, often so quickly that we don't notice it's happening.

Eliminating unnecessary distractions is essential considering the fact that it can take approximately 20 minutes to fully recover from an interruption, and how often we are interrupted (I will keep repeating that in case you were distracted the first time around.) According to a study by Gloria Mark at the University of California, Irvine, people only spent about three minutes on a task before being interrupted.[8] While it usually feels like we are being bombarded by distractions from other people, nearly half the time we are actually the ones who shift our attention to something new.[9]

It can be quite difficult to manage multiple priorities throughout the day, so coming up with a task management process is critical. A popular resource for many of my clients has been David Allen's method, described in his book *Getting Things Done*.[10]

When it comes to training your brain to focus on the task at hand, I recommend using a "turn off or tune out" philosophy. First, turn off any unnecessary "noise" that might be fighting for your brain's attention. This could be actual noise, such as a TV running in the background or conversations going on around you. I'm not suggesting you tell everyone around you to shut up, (it doesn't work well, I've tried), but you can "turn it off" by finding a more quiet environment. If you must stay put, that's when focusing exercises are going to be helpful because you will have practiced the ability to center your attention on what's important and ignore what isn't.

Distraction resistance is a way of practicing your focus by eliminating as many distractions as possible while training your brain to avoid concentrating on those that are outside of your control. The easiest way to practice distraction resistance is to make your environment "focus friendly." Turning off email rather than just minimizing it keeps us from thinking about what might be waiting for us as we see the numbers of unread emails building up.

Looking out the window or at a focus point inside your office while on a phone call will help you limit the temptation to look at your computer. Coming out from behind your desk when meeting with a co-worker not only keeps you from glancing at your monitor, but it also balances the power in the relationship and shows genuine engagement.

In his book *The Effective Executive*, Peter Drucker adds one more step to my "turn off or tune out" philosophy: - "take time out."[11] He emphasizes the need for us to give our brain time to shut down for a while, and reminds us that we do some of our best work when we're not trying to. This became very obvious to me early on in my career. I found myself having my best ideas while getting a massage. There was something about being able to totally disengage and actively work on shutting down my mind that allowed my creativity to soar. I actually started taking a notepad with me just in case (I figured this was better than asking the massage therapist to hunt for some scrap paper and a pen in my purse, which I have been known to do on occasion). Whether it was a regular therapist or someone I would only meet once, I often found myself thanking her for helping me to be creative (especially during a writing block).

Use a "Focus Phrase"

Similar to mantras, which help us focus our mind on the positive, a "focus phrase" is a word or series of words that you can use to center your mind on what's most important to you in the moment. One of my favorite examples: In the movie *For the Love of the Game*, Kevin Costner's character is pitching in a big game and being heckled quite obnoxiously (as he states, "You can always tell when you're in New York"). With the world around him in chaos, Costner says, "Clear the mechanism." At that point the sound goes away, and Costner is left with the quiet hush of his own mind, which he has trained to stay focused on only what is important in that moment. It's just him and the glove.

I no doubt identify with this film because of my experience as a softball pitcher for so many years. I remember what it was like to feel the rush of going into the game with two outs and the bases loaded while the other team cheers annoyingly. My catcher and I came up with some pretty funny sayings to help me focus on just her and the glove (I will keep those to myself to protect the innocent, and the guilty.)

I also enjoy this clip because of the phrase "clear the mechanism". As I mentioned in the introduction, the brain has often been compared to a computer. What happens when you have too many programs operating at one time? It slows down, may freeze up, and could potentially crash. What happens when there is too much on our mind? Similar results. From time to time we have to turn off our brain, reboot, and come back in order to be focused and energized.

Nowadays I use a different kind of focus phrase to help me concentrate on the present moment, whether I'm with a client, a friend, or a family member. I often tell myself, "be here, now." I recently had a client tell me about another great one: "clear and present." This individual, and his team at work, use the phrase to help them prepare before meetings. They have a quick discussion about anything that might be distracting one of the team members so that everyone is able to be fully present in the meeting. Clear the mind to be fully present for what needs to be done right here, right now.

Associating particular words or phrases with specific situations is one way we can do strength training for the brain. Each time we connect two things together in the brain, we release a chemical messenger that makes that connection stronger. If I practice deep breathing, which triggers the relaxation response in the body, while at the same time repeating the phrase "relax and refocus," I can start to associate that phrase with the response that's occurring as a result of the deep breathing. The more I practice, the stronger that association becomes, and the quicker I'm able to induce a positive state of mind with just a simple phrase.

As we repeat correlations over and over, we create a new automatic pilot. And by combining them with a desired response, you can begin to see a synergistic effect. For example, repeating the phrase "just have fun" before I do a presentation is one way I remind myself that when I have fun, I do a much better job. Then a couple of years ago I decided to add a symbol that I could see during my presentation, setting a small monkey (which represents fun to me) next to my time clock on the podium. This way, as I became wrapped up in the session, I would have an external cue to stay focused on what was most important to me in the moment – in this case, having fun – so that I would enjoy the process and not allow the stress of the situation to become too much for me to handle.

Combine both of those tricks with relaxation efforts – deep breathing, for example – and your brain will begin to automatically put all of those elements together. When I say the phrase, my brain moves my body to breathe deeply, causing me to relax faster than I used to. Seeing my symbol on the podium quickly reminds me to say the focus phrase, and the deep breathing follows. It's a cool process, and I've seen how it can directly impact my daily life. To me, this is real-world brain training.

Another example of real-world brain training happens when athletes use phrases or symbols to help put them in the right mindset for competition. Many great athletes use the power of rituals to help them train their brains and their bodies.

I recently asked my friend Justin Rose, a golfer currently on the PGA Tour, if there were any pre-shot rituals he used to help him focus on the upcoming shot. "First thing I do, to start any routine/situation, is take a deep breath. That gets me in the moment and makes anything I tell myself more meaningful," he said. The focus phrase Justin uses? "Feel the swing at target," he says. "This helps me commit to the shot rather than worry about the outcome."

The Power of the Checklist

I often hear clients expressing concerns about becoming forgetful. Many times they worry that they might be experiencing early-onset Alzheimer's disease or dementia. With so much on our plates these days, it's easy to forget things – even things that may seem unforgettable – because we are quickly moving from one thought to another in hopes of keeping up. Extraordinary performers realize that tools and systems are essential to keeping them on task, especially when there is stress involved.

The other day I was getting ready to board a plane in snowy Salt Lake City when I happened to peeSk outside and notice that the pilot was doing his checks on the outside of the plane. It was absolutely freezing, snow heavily falling, but the pilot had a process in place that had to be followed before we could board. I was comforted to see that the pilot paid such attention to the equipment – especially being the nervous flier that I am – as I recalled research I had been doing on the power of the checklist. Why do so many people try to remember everything on their own instead of using lists, processes, and systems? Those who have no choice but to be extraordinary certainly avoid this mistake. (For more information on checklists, check out *The Checklist Manifesto* by Atul Gawande.)

When I asked my good friend George Dom (former Navy air wing commander and Blue Angels flight leader) if he had some sort of image or phrase he focused on to be able to consistently perform at an incredibly high level on a daily basis (I highly recommend seeing a Blue Angel flight demo if you haven't already), he told me that there was never just one thing. Instead he used a series of pre-flight rituals and checklists to ensure all considerations were made and all relevant information was communicated. He describes this process as "entering a preflight 'bubble' ":

"The briefing room was as quiet as possible to minimize distractions, and only those participating in the mission were allowed to attend. Entering the briefing room – always a few minutes early, NEVER late – you began the process of leaving the outside world behind and beginning to draw your mind to the present. To get in synch mentally with your wingmen, and to resolve any ambiguity about the mission objectives, the plan of actions, and how we would handle 'what if?' contingencies. As we commenced the briefing, the focus and attention of everyone involved came together. Anyone who appeared disengaged stood out like a sore thumb and would be called-out on it. No compromise in having everyone's full engagement. The stakes were too high."

He went on to describe visualization exercises, stepping through each phase of the mission with graphics to enhance understanding. "No multitasking, no checking paperwork before heading to the jets. We would don our flight gear and head to the flight deck or showline without delay in order to keep our focus."

Repetition Builds Strong Habits

Using checklists and putting processes in place are great ways to start training new habits. Writing things down and planning to give focused attention to a list of action steps stimulate us to do the behavior. As George mentions in his description of his preflight routine, "Each of these checklists were embedded rituals that led us to the arena, with the window of full engagement wide open, in order to perform at our very best." Over time, that behavior becomes more automated, just like a muscle becomes stronger through physical training.

Action Plan: Focus Your Mental Energy

You can train your brain to focus your mind. How? By exercising your mental strength. Practicing full engagement is like doing exercise that builds your brain's ability to focus on what's important to you in the present moment.

Top Resistance Training/Strength Training Exercises
1. Use a Training Log

A training log is an essential part of any training program. Writing down specific steps for your plan works as a reminder and a place to track progress. Over time, steps on your training log will become automatic so that you don't have to continue to write them down, and instead you can focus on building new habits. The type of training log makes no difference. You can write it by hand, create an excel spreadsheet, or use an online tool. The important thing is that you keep it at the front of your mind and create specific rituals around how and when you will use it.

For example, I start every day by looking at my training log to remind me of what I'm working on in my life, before I look at what I need to work on for my job. Currently my focus is on having more fun and being more connected in my relationships, so checking in first thing gives me a chance to think through my plan for the day. What opportunities might come up to allow me to work on my goal, and how will I maximize them? At the end of the day I look at my training log once again to check off whether or not I have accomplished what I set out to do. On some items a simple check mark tells me that I was able to do what I wanted, and for other items I score myself on a scale of 1–5, depending on how I did. Take my vitamins – check. Practice distraction resistance – 3.5.

This ritual of checking in and out during the day has been tough to implement consistently, so I continue to research ways to make it easier. Some ideas I'm trying: putting the training log in a certain spot that I always look at (by the coffee pot maybe), putting it on top of my to-do list when I prepare the night before, or setting it in front of the door so I literally have to walk over it in order to leave at the end of the day. As I continue to practice, I find myself being more automatically driven to use the training log, a sign that I am creating a new habit. Although it's challenging, it has become clear to me that clients who use a tracking system are always more successful at accomplishing their goals. By keeping a log they keep their goals and strategies top of mind – even if they have to adapt them along the way.

Weekly Training Log							
Date: June 14 - 20, 2011							
Training Mission: To utilize tools of the SHARP program for 90 days to build new habits and reach my 90 day goals							
	Mon	Tues	Wed	Thurs	Fri	Sat	Sun
Look at training log every morning, fill in at night	X	X	X	X	X	X	X
Eat mindfullly, light and often	X	X	X	X	X	X	
Strength training 2x/week	X			X			
60 minutes of physical activity every day	X	X	X	X			X
Write min 3x/week							
ESTABLISHED RITUALS TO CONTINUE:							
Cardio 5x/week	X	X	X	X			
Mindful engagement with clients	na	X	X	X	X		
Massage at least every other week	sched nxt wk						

To download a free SHARP Training Log, visit www.synergyprograms.com.

2. Chunk Projects

Time management is an important strategy when it comes to getting things done, but it's not just the time that we need to manage. The mental energy that we give to the time that we have determines how productive that time will be. To avoid multitasking, chunk your day into time blocks so that you can focus more specifically and purposefully during that time frame. The length of time can vary, as long as you have a plan ahead of time and schedule movement breaks at least every 90 minutes to keep your focus. Breaking big projects down (chunking) into smaller steps can also help you avoid getting distracted by the big picture or feeling overwhelmed. Keep in mind that time blocks may need to get shorter as the day goes on to help manage energy and maintain focus as your energy levels are naturally declining a bit.

Sample day

8:00–8:50	Plan for the day – organize tasks by priority
8:50–9:00	Walk to Starbucks for coffee
9:00–10:30	Priority #1 task(s)
10:30–10:45	Stretching, light exercise, or morning walk
10:45–12:00	Email
12:00–12:45	Lunch away from desk/office
12:45–1:30	Priority #2 task(s)
1:30–1:45	Deep breathing, yoga, meditation, biofeedback
1:45–3:00	Priority #3 task(s)
3:00–3:15	Afternoon snack, walk stairs for 10 minutes
3:15–4:15	Priority #4 task(s)
4:15–4:30	Call a friend, watch a funny video, laugh
4:30–5:30	Priority #5 task(s), and/or wrap up for day

3. Eliminate Distractions

Avoid the big distractions by turning them off. A client once told me that when his team goes into meetings they use the "boarding door has been closed" rule, requiring anything with an on/off switch to be turned off. Not on silent mode or vibrate, but off. Even the faint sound of a phone vibrating can have anyone within hearing distance wondering who might be calling and what phone calls he or she may be missing. Some common mental-energy drainers include cell phone/blackberry/iPhone, computer monitor, background noise, bad lighting, and uncomfortable chairs. Remember – turn it off or tune it out.

What are your top mental drainers?
What distractions can you turn off?
What distractions do you need to practice tuning out?

4. *Practice Mindfulness*

Spend some time each day training yourself to be more present. It has been said that we only spend about 10% of our time in the current moment. We spend about 50% of our time anticipating what's ahead of us and 40% of our time reflecting on what's behind us. From a survival perspective this makes sense, as our focus is on preparing for the future and learning from the past. But when we want to be fully focused we need to be in the current moment, right here, right now.

I realize most people understand the benefits of mindfulness. But most also still struggle with incorporating it into their busy schedule, which is why I asked my friend Kelley McCabe, former Wall Street broker and founder of eMindful, to tell me how a busy professional can actually incorporate these strategies into an already jam-packed day.

"Take shorter periods of time," she said. "When you wake up in the morning and don't have a lot of time to sit and be mindful, set a goal: Take 100 breaths, trying to be mindful of the sensations involved with breathing (If 100 sounds daunting, as it did to me, start with 10 and gradually increase as you practice). If you get distracted, don't judge. Just come right back and focus again on your breath."

Kelley also recommended the "red dot" practice: Put stickers up in strategic places where you will be able to sneak away for a few moments to focus your mind on the here and now. Think of places where you will have uninterrupted time to take a few moments of downtime (I know there aren't many, but there is at least one I can think of). The truth is, you can be in the moment anytime – 24 hours a day. Formal practice is not required, although just like lifting weights, proper technique will help maximize your results.

Principles of mindfulness:
1. Non-judgment: becoming an impartial witness to your own experience.
2. Patience: allowing your experiences to unfold in their own time.
3. Beginner's mind: a willingness to see everything as if for the first time.
4. Trust: in your own intuition and authority and being yourself.
5. Non-striving: having no goal other than meditation itself.

6. Acceptance: of things as they actually are in the present moment.

7. Not censoring one's thoughts and allowing them to come and go.

Biofeedback (which we discussed on p. 99) is an excellent tool to assist with practicing mindfulness, as it provides immediate feedback on your ability to navigate your thoughts and emotions. It can also help busy professionals become centered because it gives you something specific to focus on, and watching the monitors change can be fun and game-like, especially for those who are more analytical in nature.

5. Play Games

As long as you have to think in order to play, games and puzzles can stimulate brain strength. If you've played the game for years, the benefit will be decreased because you start to be able to play with your "auto-brain." Make sure the games or puzzles follow the three key components of successful brain training – specific, challenging, and repetitive (more on this in Part Three).

Recap of Top Techniques for Strength Training:
1. Use a training log
2. Chunk projects
3. Eliminate distractions
4. Practice mindfulness
5. Play games

SHARP Sprints
The following are quick activities that increase mental focus:

- ### 5-minute laser focus
Chose a project or task that you've been putting off for some reason. Set a timer for 5 minutes and get as much of that task done as you can, without any disruptions. For example, the "5-Minute Room Rescue," proposed by home organizer Marla

Cilley, recommends you go to the worst room in your house and as the timer ticks down, you go to work getting things organized. When the timer alarm sounds, you can stop organizing, knowing you made some progress.[12]

- *Challenge yourself*

Think of something you usually do on automatic pilot and do it differently. For example, eat with your non-dominant hand, drive a different route to work, or shop at a different grocery store. Spend a few moments thinking through what you do during the day without much conscious effort, and mix it up.

- *Move it, move it*

Physical activity is one of the best ways to promote the strength and development of your brain. Set your timer for 1 minute, and do a quick exercise to get your heart pumping, boost brain chemicals, and circulate oxygen and glucose to your brain. Jumping jacks, squats, lunges, pushups, dips – just move. If you have more time, spend another minute or two switching up the exercises. (Check out www.powerhousehitthedeck.com for a great circuit training workout that provides a variety of intensity levels, and can be used anytime, anywhere.)

- *Count down, or up*

Choose a counting exercise, such as starting at 100 and counting down by 7s. This is a common assessment done to test concentration, focus, and attention, or what memory specialists call "registration." You can make up any counting pattern that you want, moving in any direction, as long as you have to think to do it.

- *Red dot experience*

Place a few red dot stickers in places that you will easily see during the day, and commit to increase your mindfulness, bringing your attention to the here and now, each time you notice a sticker.

Training Take-Away: What we *don't pay attention to* is just as important as what we *do pay attention to*, and being distracted by the wrong things can decrease our performance. While you might not be leading the Blue Angels in flight, when it comes to being extraordinary at what's most important to you – parent, partner, friend, leader, advisor – the stakes are always high. Training our brain to be more *focused* is *strength training* for the brain, which allows us to bring our best mental energy to the present moment.

(Find more exercises in the resources section)

STEP FIVE
Develop Resilience (flexibility training)

Flexibility Training – The Mindset Makeover

A flexible brain allows you to use your mental energy on things that move you in the direction you want to go. Our natural tendency to function in survival mode often overrides any sense of purposeful direction. Rather than just going with the flow, a flexible brain is able to adapt as needed, changing our mindset to focus on what is most important. Being able to adjust our perspective to see things in a new, more positive way impacts not only our happiness, but also improves our performance and resilience.

When it comes to cognitive health and fitness, our ability to age successfully may have more to do with our perception than any other factor. According to a study by Becca Levy and her colleagues at Yale, when it comes to healthy aging, having a positive attitude made far more difference than lowering blood pressure or reducing cholesterol, and provided more benefits than exercise, maintaining a positive weight, and not smoking. Based on the responses of more than 650 people, those who had a positive view of aging lived an average of 7.5 years longer than those who were negative about it.[1]

In her book *Counterclockwise*, Ellyn Langer describes mental flexibility as a critical element of healthy living. "I've discovered a very important truth about human psychology: Certainty is a cruel mindset. It hardens our minds against possibility and closes them to the world we actually live in."[2] Training ourselves to be more flexible allows us to stay open-minded – to think outside the box, boost creativity, and build resilience.

The Power of Perception

"We don't see things as they are, we see them as we are." —

Anaïs Nin

It's not what happens to us that ultimately forms our memories and shapes the physical structure of our brain; it's how we experience what happens to us. Unfortunately, many of us function in survival mode throughout the day, so we're not mindful of how our brains perceive what's happening around us. When we increase our awareness of how we process the world, we can develop a more positive and growth-oriented perspective, which can have a serious impact on how we respond both physically and psychologically.

Perspective is manifested in many ways through our thoughts and emotions. When we combine the various messages we tell ourselves throughout the day, we begin to develop our life "story." Over time, these messages and stories determine our mindset. In order to have a positive perspective that will support a flexible brain, we need to make sure we have the right story and that we are using a positive, growth-oriented mindset.

The Significance of Story

The messages we tell ourselves about our life are more important than what is actually happening to us. It is our perception, how we experience the world around us, that determines how we will respond. We communicate our perception both with our public voice (what we share with others) and our private voice (what we tell ourselves). As Dr. Loehr discusses in his book *The Power of Story*, "The most important story we will ever tell is the story we tell to ourselves about ourselves."[3] Each of us carries around a story that explains who we are and why we do what we do.

Our story is our internal narrative, the private comments we make to ourselves that either move us forward in the direction of what is most important to us or block us from getting where we want to go. Our internal dialogue can move us toward our goals, or pull us off course, and is often the most powerful predictor of positive change. One of the important components of identifying and rewriting our stories is our ability to "play the tape out." Often our memory is selective, recalling a faulty perception, or only a piece of the truth.

Eating a particular food, for example, can be associated with a great sense of happiness and comfort, and often that's where the story gets cut off. Playing the tape out reminds us that there is more to the story, and that behaviors also come with consequences. A trigger food sounds scrumptious until it leads to overeating. Our auto-brain drives us to consume a particular beverage, downplaying the headache that's sure to follow.

Our perceptions, emotions, and relationships are all closely shaped by how we choose to tell our story. We don't remember exact experiences, but instead we create a story that represents our interpretation or relationship to that event. Even our memory is a narrative-driven process. Everything we keep as a memory has a story connected to it, whether it be an object, a relationship, or an experience. And how we choose to store that information is not necessarily set in stone.

In fact, over time, our memories can be reframed and rewritten to best support our current state of mind, or the state of mind we aim to be in. As Michael Margolis states in his manifesto, *Believe Me*, "Something once traumatic can eventually be transformed into a 'growth experience,' or equally remain as a tragedy that forever changed one's life for the worst."[4] (Available at www.believemethebook.com)

Writing a New Story

I recently met with a friend who had to put his career aspirations on hold, yet was happier than he had ever been. I asked him to help me understand why he was so happy, even in the midst of the professional challenges he was facing.

"For the first time in my life I recognize that being really happy in all facets of your life makes you more successful, and that success is not – or should not – be defined as just a role in a company. The time will come when my children are grown, and they do not cherish the time with their father. I will be sad when that day comes, but I will also be ready for the next career challenge. For now, I choose to define success in a different manner than before. Being a great husband to my wife, being a great father to my children, and being a very productive member of our team at work is how I now define success."

He asks himself the following question when he feels as if he might be missing out on the next career opportunity: "What would you trade for 5–10 years of a wonderful family life that will leave such a lasting impression on your children?" He is happy because he has looked at his life story, and recognized that the current chapter is the one he has chosen because it's aligned with his most important values in life, as a father, a husband, and a leader.

This is not a story he re-wrote once and then forgot about. As part of his mental training, he continues to recite this message over and over to make sure it's top of mind when the doubts start creeping back. It happens to all of us. Are you prepared with the right story that is going to keep you aligned with what matters most in your life?

Strategic Scripting

Taking a story and breaking it up in to shorter messages, or scripts, can be a great way to practice a new way of thinking. One technique often used with smokers or overeaters is called counter conditioning, which uses negative associations to try to avoid particular behaviors. A new script is often used to create this shift, such as thinking about high-fat, high-sugar foods as disgusting or imagining the fats and sugars clouding arteries.

Scripts can also be used to decrease negative self-talk and increase self-efficacy. I personally use what I call my "SCAR" approach (which also reminds me that what is painful initially makes me stronger), based on my experiences as well as techniques I learned in my psychology studies. S – Stop it, C – Change it, A – Argue against it, R – Reframe it.

S – Stop it. Thought stoppage is a technique that is frequently used in cognitive therapy to eliminate negative thoughts, which are often at the root of depression and anxiety. Our negativity bias makes it easy to become overly focused on challenges and threats, which can become overwhelming – leading to distorted or obsessive thinking. Thought stoppage involves the use of a word, phrase, or action that becomes associated with the negative thought in order to stop it right away. Examples might be someone who says the word "stop," tells herself, "knock it off, now," or snaps a rubber band on his wrist (I learned this from an ex-boyfriend who used the technique on the football field). When it works, this is a quick and simple approach; however, nagging thoughts, like unwanted houseguests, don't always leave upon request.

C – Change it. A simple concept, changing a thought allows us to replace the initial negative thought with a new, more positive one. When experiencing turbulence on a plane, instead of thinking "we're going down," I now quickly tell myself to think of bumpy roads. Although it wasn't an immediate shift, the concept was easy – create a new language for a new response. While simple, the change approach can be very effective. But like thought stoppage, this technique may only scratch the surface. More complex or established thoughts may require more advanced strategies.

A – Argue against it. While it may take a greater investment of time and energy, arguing against negative thoughts can change those that feel a bit stickier and more difficult to get rid of. Identify the negative thought and write it down. Read it back to yourself and create an argument against the negative thought. For example, changing from "OMG" to "bumpy roads" was not a simple change for me. It took some convincing. I had to argue against the initial freak-out message by telling myself what everyone else tells me when I mention my fear of flying: "Air travel is the safest method of travel. You are more likely to get hurt in a car accident. Thousands of planes fly every day, and we seldom hear about issues."

R – Reframe it. Every now and then, even a good argument doesn't work. At times we have to accept that the negative thought might in fact be true. However, there are often ways of reframing what we tell ourselves to put a more positive spin on it. When I'm getting ready for a presentation and hear myself saying, "I'm freaking out," "I can't do this," or "I'm going to be sick," (yep, still happens sometimes) I reframe the situation and thought with something like "I'm excited," "I feel activation energy," or "what a rush." These statements don't change, negate, or avoid the fact that I feel a significant amount of nervous energy, but they reframe the idea of nervous energy as a positive, performance-promoting force instead of a panic-producing one.

Motivated by Mantras

Positive mantras, similar to "focus phrases," are another way to provide new language to the brain that inspires action. The simpler the mantra, the easier it is to recall in situations that may prove to be challenging or stressful. There are no rules about how to create a mantra. The key is coming up with a word or phrase that is calming, inspiring, or motivating to you, that you can call on quickly without much effort, and that focuses your mental and emotional energy in a way that is best suited for the occasion.

Athletes often use mantras to "get their head in the game" before a competition or throughout a match or event.

Individuals with high levels of stress or anxiety can find significant relief by practicing mantras, and if coupled with deep breathing practice a simple repeated phrase can stimulate the "relaxation response," which helps the body balance out the negative stress response. (For more information on the relaxation response, see Dr. Herbert Benson's book *The Relaxation Revolution*.)

The use of positive mantras has been especially beneficial to me, both personally and professionally. I've found that the use of a positive phrase such as "light and easy" helps me to stay relaxed while running marathons and half-marathons (as opposed to thinking about how heavy and slow I feel). Simple as it may sound, I credit the use of mantras for helping me to control anxiety I have struggled with for most of my life, particularly around public speaking and flying. Reminding myself that the pre-speaking nervous energy actually helps me bring my best self to the stage has enabled me to keep from stressing myself out to the point that I won't go on. Although the nerves are still there, my perspective has changed which has significantly decreased the impact of stress on my system.

There are a lot of great ways you can use mantras during the day to help create the right story for yourself, increase resilience, and motivate you toward your goal. I asked my financial advisor, who also happens to be an Ironman, what motivates him to take on such a lofty physical challenge in the midst of a hectic work schedule, keeping a healthy marriage, and having an active family life. "If you set a goal – no matter how large or unattainable it may seem to other people – if you commit yourself to it and are willing to work hard to achieve it, you can do anything!" he said. "Teaching my children this lesson is one of my main motivations, and it is what I think about when I become physically or mentally exhausted. After all is said in done, the famous Ironman mantra really is the key to getting through many of life's adversities:

Pain is temporary...quitting lasts forever!"

Mantras may be simple, but they are powerful if you can come up with a word or phrase that is positive and meaningful to you, and that you practice consistently. Remember that each time we repeat a mantra, our brain fires chemicals to help strengthen neural connections, making our new way of thinking more automatic.

Repeat a mantra every time your mind is not required to be engaged in something important, such as while traveling on a bus or a train, waiting in line, walking, etc., (but not while driving or crossing a street). You may also repeat them in special sessions of 2–3 minutes each several times a day. Relax any physical, emotional, or mental tension while affirming. The stronger the concentration and the more faith you have in what you are doing, the better the results will be.

Examples of Positive Mantras
- I am healthy and happy.
- I have a lot of energy.
- I study and comprehend fast.
- My mind is calm.
- I am calm and relaxed in every situation.
- My thoughts are under my control.
- I radiate love and happiness.
- I am surrounded by love.
- I have a wonderful and satisfying job.
- Things just keep getting better.

Mindset Matters
Our mindset is the overarching theme of our story, or the lens through which we look at life. In her book *Mindset: The New Psychology of Success*, Carol Dweck of Stanford University states that our mindset is based on our beliefs about our most basic qualities and abilities. Dweck separates mindset into two fundamental categories, a growth mindset and a fixed mindset. Someone who believes that intelligence is a fixed trait – either you have it or you don't – is considered to be of a fixed mindset. These individuals tend to believe that success is based

on talent, and may be quick to dismiss effort and hard work as being for the weak or less intelligent.[5]

With a fixed mindset, people often opt for easier tasks that require less effort, and they may give up quickly. Whether it's work-related or an important relationship, fixed mindset people will often throw in the towel faster than someone who believes he has the ability to work hard for change.

With a growth mindset, difficulties are seen as opportunities for growth. People with a growth mindset are more willing to take risks, put in extra effort without feeling stupid, and recognize the benefit of learning, regardless of outcome. They believe they can develop their brains, abilities, and talents. In her research, Dweck found that individuals trained on a growth mindset pursue goals related to learning and not just performance.

Multiple studies show that a growth mindset is beneficial in business. Negotiators with a growth mindset are more able to push past obstacles and reach a mutually beneficial agreement. Business school students who were taught a growth mindset learned more skills and received better grades in their negotiation class. Leaders may benefit from a growth mindset because they are better equipped to coach and develop their employees, and are quicker to notice improvement in their team than leaders with a fixed mindset.

Having an optimistic or positive mindset has serious benefits, both in and out of the office. Studies show that a positive mindset has a significant impact on cognitive functioning in areas such as attention, intuition, and creativity. Being positive helps speed up the recovery from cardiovascular problems, lowers cortisol, reduces the inflammatory effect of stress, and improves the chance of living a long, healthy life. According to Barbara Friedrickson at the University of North Carolina and author of the book *Positivity*, positive affect also produces future health and well being.[6]

Many times our automatic response takes control in challenging situations, and we fail to recognize that there is a choice in the story we tell ourselves. The voice we choose to listen to ultimately directs our behavior. Although our mindset may seem to be something we're just born with, the reality is different. Brain plasticity means that we have the ability to choose a new story, and when we practice this new way of responding over and over again we create a new way of thinking and a more positive automatic response. We will discuss ways to rewrite your story and makeover your mindset, but first let's look at the reason so many of us get stuck with "stinkin' thinkin'" in the first place.

Negativity Bias – "Survival Mode"

As human beings designed with excellent survival instincts, we have a built-in bias that causes us to focus more on the negatives around us than the positives. While positive things are wonderful, if we are worried about survival they mean very little when compared to the saber-tooth tiger staring us in the face (literally or figuratively).

When we experience negative, "fight or flight" emotions, our focus narrows in on the things that seem dangerous. According to Fredrickson's "Broaden and Build" theory, positive emotions lead us to see the world around us with a wider perspective. They allow us to focus on things such as building relationships, collaborating with others, and thinking outside the box. Positive emotions broaden the scope of our attention and increase our ability to use different elements of our cognitive functioning.[7] They widen the lens through which we see the world around us, enabling us to connect more dots, which enhances our ability to be creative.

These emotions flood our brain with endorphins that not only make us feel good but also improve "mental muscle." Dopamine, for example, is released in the brain when we experience pleasure, and it helps build stronger neural pathways. Positive emotions also seem to have a significant impact on our overall health and well-being. When we are happy, our immune system functions better, making us quicker to recover from injury or illness.

SHARP Science: Prospective studies have shown that a positive mindset improves our resilience,[8] increases happiness,[9] decreases cortisol, reduces inflammation,[10] reduces pain,[11] and decreases our risk of stroke.[12]

Challenge vs. Threat

When we are functioning in a state of "survival," our thoughts are fixated on the things that will help protect us from our biggest threats. A simple example: the difficulty most people have controlling food portions. From an evolutionary perspective, our greatest threat is running out of resources, in particular the energy we need to survive. Although we are all aware that there is no food shortage, our brain still functions as if there might be in the near future. Which means the brain often encourages us, through hormones and other brain chemicals related to appetite, to consume as much food as possible when it's available. We also are wired to move as little as possible in order to protect the energy stores we already have.

In monitoring brain activity, we can see that particular hormones are released when the brain feels threatened, and this could be in response to both an actual threat or a perceived threat. So even if we logically know that there is plenty of food available, the perception that is created by eating sporadically causes the brain to respond as if it has run out of food.

If the food products we do eat lack critical nutrients, our brain perceives that same type of threat – an energy shortage. In order to decrease energy going out and increase energy coming in, our metabolism slows down, appetite is increased, and we eat more food. This basic desire gets neurons firing in the brain to activate our behavior, and the more often it happens the more automatic our response becomes, which is why some people feel completely out of control when it comes to eating habits.

With a more mindful approach, we design a strategy that helps us stick to our game plan, and keeps stress controlled enough to allow the brain to function optimally. This way, we realize there is no threat and our body is able to function at it's best.

Interestingly, the sense of threat brings about a chemical response in the brain that is much different from the one triggered when we experience something we consider a challenge. Physiological responses to a threat include increased blood pressure, blood sugar, and adrenaline, which helps to explain why a tendency to evaluate stressful situations as a threat increases the risk of developing heart disease. When we perceive a situation as challenging, we believe that we have the resources necessary to handle the situation, and everything changes.

Look at what happens internally, and you will see a very different set of chemicals being released in the body in a challenging situation because a challenge is something that appears to be temporary. The body responds physically in a way that it would during an acutely stressful situation. We need to do something different, and so we do – and then move on. When we experience a threat, however, our mental and physical responses change. In this case, we are not sure if we have the resources to manage the situation. The chemical response in the body is more like the one associated with chronic stress: Toxic stress hormones remain in the body for a longer period of time and therefore create more damage.

SHARP Science: A study of 7,400 employees found that people who believed they had little control over deadlines imposed by other people had a 50% higher risk of coronary heart disease than their counterparts. Who would have imagined that lacking a sense of control is just as risky for heart disease as high blood pressure?[13]

In order to decrease the negative impact of stress in our lives, we need to develop a mindset that enables us to see stress as a challenge, not a threat. We can retrain our brain by using flexibility exercises so that we will have more control over how we perceive and respond to the world around us. According to

David Kessler in his book *The End of Overeating*, "To control our brains, we have to be mistrustful of our brains. We have to recognize they are the vehicle to invite us to do things that at some point in our evolutionary past may have been very useful, but have gotten completely out of control."[14]

The Power of Mind – You Have More Control Than You Think

Fortunately, we can train our mind to think differently and see life through a more positive lens. Multiple studies have shown that using techniques such as journaling, listing things we're grateful for, and sending thank-you notes to others can actually train our brain to be more optimistic. Experts in the field of positive psychology have discovered that the advantages of being happy extend well beyond just feeling better, but actually impact our health and our performance.

Positive psychology is not just about seeing life through rose-colored glasses. At first glance, many people dismiss the idea of happiness training because they assume that our level of happiness is something ingrained in our personality or determined by our genes. Wrong. It turns out that our circumstances have much less to do with our happiness than our state of mind. According to positive-psychologist Sonja Lyubomirsky in her book, *The How of Happiness*, research suggests that up to 40 percent of our happiness might stem from intentional activities – those we choose to engage in.[15]

What's very surprising to most people is that only about 10% has to do with life circumstances. Waiting to hit the lottery to be happy doesn't make sense, and, in fact, lottery winners may end up being worse off in the long run. Their happiness not only quickly fades back to their status quo, but the winners also have added pressure and responsibility from their financial gains. Practicing positive thinking is like exercise that builds your brain's ability to focus on what's good in life, right here and now. More than just putting you in a better mood, this type of "mindset makeover" has been shown to significantly benefit performance in many aspects of life.

SHARP Science: A study by Lyubomirsky and her colleagues revealed compelling evidence that positive affect fosters the following resources, skills, and behaviors: sociability and activity, altruism, liking of self and others, strong bodies and immune systems, effective conflict resolution skills and original thinking.[16]

Sometimes just thinking that something good is going to happen causes us to have a positive outcome. In a groundbreaking study by Alia Crum and Ellen Langer in 2007, a group of hotel maids were told about the many benefits of exercise. When the maids were first interviewed, 67 percent of them reported that they did not exercise regularly. Crum and Langer were curious to find out if there would be any effect on the maids if they were told that they were already doing enough exercise to get more than the daily recommendations.

Half of the group were given a document describing the health benefits of exercise and told that they worked hard enough to receive those benefits. They were also given estimates of how many calories they were burning in each of their activities: 40 calories for changing bed linens for 15 minutes, 100 calories for 30 minutes of vacuuming, and so on. The other group of maids were given documentation on the health benefits of exercise, but not told that their typical daily routine was giving them enough activity to reap those benefits.

After four weeks, the researchers checked in with the study participants and found that the group who had been told they were good exercisers had lost an average of 1.8 pounds, or nearly a half pound a week, while the other group had not lost an ounce. In order to determine the cause of the weight loss, the researchers looked at any possible variables and determined that the participants hadn't changed their diet in any meaningful way, and they weren't working more hours or sneaking off to the gym.[17]

We've all heard of the placebo effect. When people think they're getting some sort of health benefit or medical treatment, they often feel better because their mind tells them they should feel better. Whether or not the placebo effect was in force in this study, or the information given to the maids who lost weight triggered more awareness of other healthy choices throughout the day, the fact is that believing they were doing something good for themselves gave the hotel maids a beneficial outcome without any additional conscious effort.

Positivity is Powerful

It turns out that people in a positive mood have many advantages over those who are negative or neutral, including mental flexibility. According to Lyobomirsky, "People in a positive mood are more likely to have richer associations with existing knowledge structures (things we already have committed to memory), and thus are more likely to be more flexible and original.[16] Martin Seligman, often called the "Godfather" of positive psychology, believes that positive people are more resilient because when difficulties strike they are able to perform better, and their physical health is stronger.

> *SHARP Science: Training programs that focus on optimism show increased outcome expectations, self efficacy, motivation, learning, and transfer when compared to standard training.[18]

Barbara Fredrickson has studied the power of positivity in companies that she has researched and consulted with. Fredrickson and her team analyze the words that are said in business meetings in order to determining their "positivity ratio," or the ratio of positive to negative statements. According to Fredrickson, companies with a positivity ratio higher than 2.9:1 (or 2.9 positive statements for every 1 negative statement) are flourishing. Below that ratio, companies don't seem to be doing well economically. But Fredrickson warns us not to go overboard with compliments, as anything above 13:1 may cause you to lose your credibility.[19]

SHARP Science: Relationship expert John Gottman looked at the positivity ratio in the conversations between married couples. He found that in relationships, a 2.9:1 ratio of positive to negative statements is not enough to make a successful, flourishing partnership. To reach that goal, couples need a 5:1 ratio of positive to negative – or five positive statements for every one critical statement. Gottman suggests that a 2.9:1 ratio means you are headed for divorce, and a habit of 1:3 is an "unmitigated catastrophe."[20]

One of the quickest ways to boost happiness is to appreciate what you already have in your life. Positive psychologists recommend simple gratitude exercises that give you the opportunity to scan the world around you to see what is going well, which helps train the brain to focus more on the good things than the bad.

In a study on gratitude writing, participants who wrote down three good things each day for a week were happier at one-, three-, and six-month follow-ups.[21] Gratitude writers not only feel happier, they also exercise more often, report fewer physical complaints, and exhibit more helpful behavior towards friends and neighbors.[22]

We all know people who always seem to see the world through rose-colored glasses, and that might not work for you. Being optimistic doesn't mean being unrealistic, but training your brain to see positive things more regularly will help you create a more beneficial mindset.

Cultivate Creativity

One big reason that a flexible brain is so important in life is that it enables us to think outside the box. Creativity requires a healthy imagination. As children, we were encouraged to use our imagination, dream big, and see life as a playful adventure. But somewhere along the way, someone told us to be realistic, grow up, and act like adults (how boring). Yet creativity is not only an important trait to have in our personal life, it's critical for most business professionals.

Creativity helps us stand out from the competition when it comes to promoting ourselves and our business. We can strengthen important client relationships by utilizing creativity to create what my friend John Evans, Executive Director at Janus Labs, calls "Wow moments" – when a client is delighted by an act that is thoughtful and meaningful to them personally. According to John, these exchanges are important because they "draw energy to the products or services we provide and makes for a more delightful company culture." John adds, "of course, the great hinge for this to happen starts with creativity." He recommends making a list of the top relationships you want to "Wow", and identifying two or more passions for each. Then give yourself a specific time frame in which to "Wow" each one of them.

My friend Dana Klein once told me about an experience he had with a hotel he had to call his second home for a while, when he was commuting for work.

"I had been staying at the JW Marriott in Cherry Creek [Colorado] regularly for a couple of years or so, as it was connected to the building of the company I worked for at the time. Around 1997, Marriott moved to upgrade their bedding with nicer sheets, comforters, and pillows. However, in their infinite wisdom someone decided to give their guests more pillows across the bed. In order to do this they had to make their pillows smaller. While aesthetically this looks really neat, they aren't much bigger than a throw pillow on your couch.

Each night I would wake up and my head would be off the pillow, and I wasn't getting a good night sleep. After a couple of months of this, I got one of those email surveys titled "How was your stay." Well, this was just the opportunity to unload. I gave the hotel generally good marks because other than the bed everything is usually terrific. When it came time to grade the room and the bedding, I gave them a 2 out of 10, and the 2 was because there was a bed in the room.

About two weeks later I got a message from the hotel's general manager, Dani Stern – the best hotelier I've ever met – and he wanted to know what he could do to help me feel better about my stay. My response was that there probably wasn't much he could do, as I was sure that someone back at Marriott headquarters had specified those pillows and they either never slept at a Marriott or their head was the size of a pin. Dani assured me that he would do everything he could to make my upcoming stays more enjoyable. I told him all in all things were fine, and he could continue to rely on me to be a happy, albeit tired, guest at his hotel.

On my very next trip to the JW, about a week later, I had the usual efficient check-in and greetings, but when I got up to my room waiting for me on my bed were TWO KING SIZED PILLOWS, with my name embroidered on each one!!! I could not have been more ecstatic – what an incredibly thoughtful gift. Fortunately, I had a brand new camera I had brought along to test out on this trip, so some of the first pictures I took were of MY pillows. To this day, I still tell the story of those pillows, and what a fabulous hotel the JW Marriott in Cherry Creek is."

For my friend Dana, this was a huge "Wow" moment, even though it cost the hotel very little to make it happen. And I've heard him tell this story many, many times – nothing sells your business better than a happy client.

Not only does creativity help us to find ways to "Wow" the people we care about, it also allows us to be more open-minded and flexible. This enables us to see different perspectives and make more thoughtful decisions that incorporate the best of what the team brings to the table. Boosting positive thinking increases our ability to be creative because it allows us to focus on what's going well, instead of becoming narrowly focused on what's going wrong. When you're in a bad mood, your tendency is to fall back on what you already know in a defensive manner, as opposed to gathering ideas and insight from other people and weighing all of the options.

A quick way to boost creativity is to spend a few minutes exercising our mental flexibility through positivity training. Positive-psychologists have discovered several strategies to boost optimism. Something as simple as writing down three things you're grateful for every morning can help train your brain to scan the world for positive things, instead of always focusing on the negative ones.

The activity that seems to be most beneficial (meaning the greatest boost in positivity) is writing a letter of thanks to someone you appreciate. If possible, read the letter aloud to that person. If that is not an option, you will still personally experience a happiness boost just by expressing yourself, even if you're the only one who will ever read it.

> *SHARP Science:* Positive mood has been shown to produce broader attention, more creative thinking, and more holistic thinking. This is in contrast to negative mood, which produces narrowed attention.[23]

Action Plan: Flexibility Training

You can train your brain to see things more positively by exercising your mental flexibility. When you write down the positive things that happen in your day, your brain is forced to focus on good times. You scan your day looking for those things that brought you joy. The more often you do this type of "soul searching," the more your brain releases chemicals that make the positive connections stronger, based on the "use it or lose it" principle of brain plasticity.

Soon, focusing on the positive becomes your new automatic pilot mode. Because our brain can only focus on one thing at a time, paying attention to the positive leaves little energy to spend on the negative. Over time, that change gives us a more positive lens through which we view our lives.

Top Techniques for Training Mental Flexibility

1. Get Your Story Right

*(Adapted from *The Power of Story*, by Dr. Jim Loehr) This exercise for re-writing your story includes three steps: Recognize it, rewrite it, and recite it.

In order to create the right story, you must first recognize what story you're currently using so that you can change it. Dr.

Loehr calls this our "old story" and states that every negative habit in our life inevitably comes with a story that supports it.[3] When you think of something you want to do differently, and you say to yourself ("I would like to _____), there is usually a "but" that quickly follows. Otherwise we'd already be doing it. (My friends and I refer to this as the "Big But.") That reasoning allows us to continue feeling OK about the fact we aren't doing what we want to be doing, at least temporarily, and is the basis for the "old story" that needs to be changed. For example, I may say that "I want to travel less," but I am quick to explain why that isn't possible: "BUT… If I'm not on the road I'm not making money, so I'd better re-pack my bags."

Once we recognize the story we're telling ourselves, we can rewrite it in a more positive way to help us move in the direction of what we are trying to accomplish. This is done by taking a hard look at why the new behavior is so important to us, and identifying the consequences of not making the change. Using the same example above, it might sound something like this:

> "I want to travel less because I want to build more solid connections with my friends and community. If I continue to travel this much I will become more disconnected, and it will negatively impact my health, physically and emotionally. The truth is, there may be some other projects I can pick up that would allow me to work closer to home, whether it's exploring new clients or doing more writing assignments."

After we rewrite our story, it is critical that we practice telling ourselves the new story on a regular basis. Repetition is essential to create new ways of thinking. Remember, we are trying to establish and strengthen new pathways in the brain, which takes work. Over time, however, the new path will be the preferred path, and our automatic thoughts will be the ones that are more supportive of where we want to go.

Recognize it: What messages are you currently telling yourself that might be getting in the way of your progress?

Rewrite it: What could you say to yourself that would be more positive, moving you in the direction of your goals?

Recite it: Read the new story back to yourself, read it out loud, and repeat it often.

2. Practice Gratitude

According to multiple studies, people who keep a daily gratitude list feel more optimistic, exercise more frequently, and report fewer physical complaints. They also experience more positive emotions and fewer negative emotions, and exhibit more helpful behavior towards friends and neighbors.[22] Each morning, take a moment to write down three things you're grateful for. Or if you'd prefer to experience gratitude in the evenings before bed, try "counting your blessings" – list or journal about what went well today. For an even greater positivity boost, exchange blessings lists with your partner or spouse.

What are three things you are grateful for right now?

1.

2.

3.

You may want to start a "blessings journal," in which you keep track of your gratitude lists in one place so you can have the opportunity to go back through them when you aren't feeling quite as grateful. We all have times when we experience the blues, or find ourself in a funk, so having a journal to remind us of what matters most and the many blessings we have in our life can help boost our sense of gratitude in the midst of difficult times.

Another way to practice gratitude is to write a gratitude letter. Think of someone who has contributed to your well-being, someone whom you've never fully thanked. Write a letter to that person describing the benefits you have received. Be detailed. Describe how the actions made you feel. Take this letter and read it aloud to that person, and if possible, do this in person so you can be together to exchange emotions.

If you are unable to deliver your message in person, you will still benefit from the experience because you are able to express how you feel, if only to yourself.

3. Makeover Your Mindset

You can create a new mindset by learning to focus on the positive and being open to different ways of thinking. Writing is an excellent way to get a better sense of your current mindset and make adjustments so that you can see things from a new perspective. Spend a few minutes writing about a challenging situation you're currently dealing with. Don't censor what you're writing – just let it flow freely. When you have written as much as you have to say for now, ask yourself the following questions about your circumstances:

1. What is the significance of the current circumstances?
2. What kind of sense can you make of these circumstances?
3. Have you reminded yourself how much worse things could be?
4. Have you thought about how this event could change your life in a positive way?
5. Can you envision anything good that might come out of dealing with this challenge?

This exercise is not intended to make you ignore or belittle the challenges you have or to encourage you to be unconsciously optimistic about them, but rather to help you look for meaning and positive outcomes that could occur in order to help promote positive emotions as you confront challenges.

4. Meditate

Of all the mind-body practices, meditation takes the prize for the most research currently available to validate its benefits in multiple dimensions – body, mind, and spirit.

There are many ways to use meditation techniques for mental flexibility. A focusing exercise is considered meditation if it:

- utilizes a specific and clearly defined technique
- involves muscle relaxation somewhere during the process
- involves logic relaxation (i.e., not "to intend" to analyze the possible psychophysical effects, not "to intend" to judge the possible results, and not "to intend" to create any type of expectation regarding the process)
- is a self-induced state
- involves the use of a self-focus skill or "anchor" for attention

Mantra meditation – These are meditation practices in which a main element of practice is a positive mantra such as the Relaxation Response technique (Relaxation Response or RR), the Transcendental Meditation® technique, Clinically Standardized Meditation (CSM), Acem meditation, and Ananda Marga, to name a few.

Mindfulness meditation – Though described slightly differently by Eastern and Western interpreters, this type of meditation refers generally to practices that cultivate awareness, acceptance, and non-judgment, and require paying attention to the present moment. Examples include Mindfulness-Based Stress Reduction (MBSR), Mindfulness-Based Cognitive Therapy (MBCT), Vipassana meditation, Zen Buddhist meditation, and other types of meditation that focus on the practice of mindfulness.

Tai Chi – Often called "meditation in motion," Tai Chi is a Chinese martial art characterized by soft, slow, flowing movements that emphasize force and complete relaxation.

Yoga – There are a broad group of techniques rooted in yogic tradition that incorporate postures, breath control, and meditation. Specific practices include Hatha yoga, Kundalini yoga, and individual components of Yoga such as pranayama (breath control exercises).

Guided Imagery – It can be very difficult for people to slow down their mind enough to meditate when they're used to going a million miles an hour. Using a guided imagery CD can help walk you through the process of relaxation and center your mental energy on the here and now (for a sample guided imagery track, go to www.synergyprograms.com).

There are no set "rules" for how or when to practice meditation. The key is that you schedule it into your day and try to keep your practice consistent so that you can rely on the techniques when you need them most.

5. Use Signature Strengths in New Ways

Honesty. Loyalty. Perseverance. Creativity. Kindness. These are some of the character strengths that are valued across all cultures. Positive-psychology experts believe that you can get more satisfaction out of life if you identify which of these character strengths you have in abundance and then use them as much as possible at work, in hobbies, and with friends and family.

One of the exercises Dr. Seligman uses when he works with soldiers to help build their emotional resilience is to have them write a story of "strengths in challenge." Once you identify your strengths, think about experiences you've had in your life that have been difficult, and how your personal strengths helped you get through.

1. Discover Your Strengths: Take the VIA survey of strengths to assess your top five strengths, and think of ways to use those strengths more in your daily life. (Go to www.authentichappiness.com)

2. Write about a challenging time and how your signature strengths helped you overcome the challenge. Discuss how going through the "storm" actually made you stronger, and what lessons you learned that you can apply to your life moving forward.

Use your strengths intentionally by finding more ways to use them throughout your day. Seligman recommends finding time in your schedule to commit to exercising a signature strength in a new way, either at work or at home. For example, use your creativity to take photographs and make a collage. If you appreciate beauty, go for a long walk and try to be mindful of your surroundings, fully taking in the scenery. After using your strength, journal about your experience. Describe how you felt before, during, and after the activity. Discuss plans to use this activity again, or come up with a new activity to try to utilize another signature strength at the next opportunity.

Recap of Top Techniques for Flexibility Training:
1. Get your story right
2. Practice gratitude
3. Makeover your mindset
4. Meditate
5. Use signature strengths in new ways

SHARP Sprints

The following are quick activities that increase mental flexibility:

- *Thank-you notes*

Jot a quick note to a family member, friend, colleague, or even someone you just met, to show your appreciation.

- *Visualization*

Think through something that you want to practice, and visualize in as much detail what it would feel like, look like, sound like. Use as many senses as possible to help provide a true-to-life mental experience.

- *Short guided imagery*

It can be difficult to focus on relaxation when your mind is being pulled a million different directions. Guided imagery provides step-by- step instructions for you to follow in order to reach a desired state of mind.

- *Look back and forth*

Gratitude doesn't have to be just about what's already happened. Write down some things you are grateful for that occurred in the past, and then fast forward, just a little bit, and write down what you're looking forward to.

- *Rewrite a short story*

When dealing with a challenging situation, quickly write down bullet points that are negative and see if you can reframe them in a more positive way. Recall a time one door closed but another one opened.

Training Take Away: What we *perceive* is what we *experience*, and focusing on the wrong thing can completely change what we see... literally. As the great psychologist William James once said, "My experience is what I agree to attend to." Developing a *positive, growth-oriented, opportunity-based* mindset is *flexibility training* for the brain, which allows us to be resilient in complex situations and to see the positive in even the most challenging circumstances.

(Find more exercises in the resources section)

STEP SIX
Make it Last (endurance training)

Endurance Training – Sustaining Strength and Resilience

Having a resilient brain allows you to enjoy successful, healthy aging. We all know that as we age, our body and brain functioning naturally decline. But with the proper training we can prolong the use of a strong, flexible mind over time. With the right regimen in place, our brain health and cognitive fitness efforts may even prevent age-related disease and dementia.

In the anti-aging research, it has been widely accepted that staying sharp requires that the structure of the neurons and their connections in the brain stay strong, and that we have a flexible mindset in order to decrease the negative impact of stress and maximize the benefits of positivity.

Maintaining and Training Memory

If you've ever wondered if you might be losing your mind, you are not alone. Even at a young age, most of us experience some forgetfulness. Weak memory can be situational, due to poor nutrition, or even a lack of movement (sitting too long). Oftentimes, temporary memory loss or mental fogginess can be caused by lack of sleep, alcohol consumption, or medication. It can also be circumstantial, based on an overload of work or other activities, or too many distractions. We've all had a moment when we walked into a room and wondered why we were there, spent way too much time searching for our car keys, or found our cell phone in the fridge (or is that just me?).

However, memory loss can be a sign of weak brain strength or flexibility, which is why endurance training requires a combination of both. Memory can also be a symptom of brain disease, and although the research is limited, experts agree that brain training exercises have the potential to decrease the risk of developing Alzheimer's or other forms of dementia. And keep in mind what I mentioned earlier in the strength training section: A stronger, more flexible brain may mean that someone with Alzheimer's plaques and tangles will never experience a single symptom.

As I researched memory for this book, I quickly realized that there was a lot more to maintaining memory than I initially thought. My association with memory up to this point had been all about healthy aging, based on my personal focus on learning more about preventing Alzheimer's. However, memory is not something we just want to maintain. It's something we can train to improve immediately – and probably should.

In any business it's important to stand out from the competition, and often the best way to do that is based on the relationship you create with your clients. For example, in the financial services business, such relationships are definitely a critical part of business development. When I consider what is most important to me in choosing an advisor, whether it is for my finances, health, or the development of my own business, the key element is always the relationship – how I feel with the other person. An advisor who is able to remember not only my name but also things that are important to me (family names, experiences, investment preferences, personal and professional goals, etc.) is a person who can earn my business.

I witnessed firsthand how a strong memory can benefit the development of new relationships when I worked at my previous job. My colleague, Chris Jordan, would always begin his lecture on exercise by asking the clients to turn over their name tags. He then would go around the room and state each person's first name – often with groups of up to 40 people at a time. Chris not only remembered their names the first day, but he continued to call them by name in the gym on days two and three, when they were no longer wearing name tags. He also was able to commit to memory the target heart rate zone for each individual, as he went around the room and reminded each person of where his or her heart rate should be when working out. Although I watched him do this for years, I was always impressed.

I recently had a chance to talk to Chris about this feat. I asked if he intentionally practiced this skill in order to strengthen his relationships with the clients, or if it was something that just came naturally to him. "I was able to recognize a certain strength I had for organization and utilize it to make a connection with my clients," Chris explained. In the program feedback, it was very common to hear the clients say, "even though I was in a group, you made me feel like an individual." And although I can testify that the impact was significant, try as I may, I have never been able to develop this strength.

Because I knew Chris was a super-organized "nerd" (to use his words) and I was much more of a "social butterfly" (to use the words of a college friend of mine), I stopped trying to master this skill almost immediately. But talking to Chris about his process reminded me that even though we have genetic pre-dispositions for different things (which is why my parents took me out of gymnastics quickly), if we have the right approach and practice consistently, we can do things we never thought possible (except maybe gymnastics, in my case).

I haven't given up on my memory quite yet though. In fact, I've put together a memory muscle-building workout for myself that I'm sharing with you in the resources section of this book in case you want to try it out. (Let me know if it works.)

Mind Over Matter

While my memory is still a work in progress, there are a few other things I've been able to do in my life that I never imagined would be possible. I've discussed a few of them in previous sections when I talked about my stories and personal mantras. The fact that I've been able to overcome my fears of flying and public speaking has allowed me to follow a career path I never dreamed possible (you can read more about my story in the conclusion). Mind over matter is more than just "snapping out of something." We can accomplish amazing things when we train our brain to be stronger and more flexible, especially when our goals are tied to our deepest values and beliefs. When we are fueled by our purpose, there are few limitations to what we can accomplish.

I'd like to share a story from a previous client, David, a family wealth director in Winter Park, Florida, who has used this type of real-world brain training to accomplish things he never thought possible – things that go far beyond overcoming phobias. You will notice that David has a perspective focused on what's most important to him, and flexible enough to see the good in challenging situations.

I was lucky enough to have suffered a potentially life threatening accident over 25 years ago, which left me with an artificial hip, thirteen pins, and a metal plate. They thought I may be a paraplegic, then thought I may never walk again, then told me I would not play competitive sports... I still remember the first day I could get up in the hospital and make it to the door of my hospital room and see a young grandchild walking along with his grandmother, and he said, "look, granny, he has a walker just like you!" I remember thinking bad thoughts about that kid.

I have been very fortunate in many aspects of my life and then have had to battle through others such as the accident. My sister passed away at the age of 38 after battling leukemia for almost six years, and then my best friend growing up was killed in a horrific accident very shortly after that. This was part of the reason I felt the need to reconnect with myself and my family. I had the opportunity to go through a one-on-one program with Dr. Loehr, and it was like a light bulb being turned on. It really helped me understand the meaning of full engagement and how balance in your life is key.

Part of that balance is what you talk about in your book: "upgrading your life's personal operating system." Getting some of the training and having the opportunity to better understand how your body works and how important the balances are have helped me tremendously in my personal and professional career.

Last year my other best friend growing up also passed away from cancer, and just this past September I suffered a ruptured C6-C7 and underwent spinal fusion.

So I think as much as your SHARP Strategies are key and vital to boost your brainpower and excel in your chosen life, they can also be a key to uncovering or discovering powers within yourself to push you to succeed.

I just ran my third Boston Marathon three weeks ago with all of my pins, plates, clips, fusions, etc. Your brain is a power tool that if trained properly can "will you" to accomplish pretty much anything and understand what is really important in life.

I agree with Winifred Gallaher, author of *Rapt*, when she says that "your quality of life is determined by your choice of where you choose to focus your attention."[1] When we are focused on what matters most to us, we can do things we never thought possible.

The Power of Purpose

A sense of connection to the world around us is critical to fostering longevity, and that connection goes beyond developing good personal relationships. A sense of purpose beyond merely survival is at the core of what makes us human. We function best when we are on a mission that truly matters, and we can all agree that when we're doing something that we believe in, we are always more on our game.

In one of my favorite books, *The Power of Purpose*, Robert Leider sought to discover what people would do differently if they had the chance to do it all over again.[2] The book was developed by interviewing older adults (over age 65) about some of the most important questions in life. According to Leider, there were three themes that wove their way through all the interviews.

The older adults consistently said that if they could live their lives over again, they would:

Be more reflective.
Be more courageous.
Be clear earlier about purpose.

There is nothing in those statements about spending more time in the office, making more money, being more famous, having more power, or any of the things that younger people often strive for. Purpose is the driving force behind everything we do, and with the right sense of purpose (unique to each individual), we can accomplish things we never dreamed possible. Maybe more importantly, we can accomplish those things and feel proud of what we've done, knowing that it was done on purpose.

When purpose is discussed in the office, it's usually through some sort of corporate mission or vision statement. Yet, for the individual workers, there is often a disconnect between what is important to them personally and what the organization claims to stand for. Leider suggests, "the failure of many organizations to enlist people in some kind of unselfish, non-quantitative purpose is at the root of many productivity problems today. When we ignore purpose at work, we inhibit the highest motivator."

Purpose is also what drives our day-to-day behaviors, whether we realize it or not. Each day we are forced to answer the question, "why do I get up in the morning?" It is important to face this challenge on a regular basis to make sure that we are living in a way that is in harmony with our deepest values and beliefs.

Keep in mind that all of us go through times when we feel lost and lacking in direction. Purpose is not something we decide once and forget. It is important to make connecting to a purpose a part of our daily routine by building habits that make us take a look, on a regular basis, at what matters most. You might write your mission statement or personal vision on a Post-it Note and put it on your mirror, put a photo of people you care about on your screensaver, or play a song that inspires you at a strategic time of the day (or even better, make it your ringtone, as I did, so you hear it throughout the day).

A client in a recent workshop shared with me that he has a poem he recites to himself anytime he feels disconnected from his life's purpose. This is another reason why training memory is important: We can keep special people, impactful messages, and inspiring words close by to pull from our mental files whenever we need to plug back into purpose.

Start With Your Foundation and Cross Train

Research has suggested that less than 50 percent of our memory and brain function is inherited – which leaves a lot of room for us to control how our brain ages. Some experts believe that lifestyle-related issues such as obesity, diabetes, hypertension, smoking, sedentary lifestyle, high cholesterol, and chronic stress have the potential to increase the risk of developing cognitive impairment as much as 16-fold – a far greater risk than having a parent with Alzheimer's disease.[3]

The *SYNERGY Fab 5* healthy living strategies are critical to keeping your brain healthy and strong over time. One way to fuse brain health and brain training together is to cross train your body and mind within the same activity – giving you a greater return on your time and energy investment.

A great example: laughing more during the day. Laughter is such great medicine that laughter therapy, groups, and clubs have sprouted out all over the country to help people improve their health and happiness. It's a bit sad to think that we have to designate specific laughing time, but just like everything else we've talked about so far, if you don't plan it, it's not going to happen. Yes, we may laugh during the day from time to time, but because we are so busy, most of us hardly slow down long enough to allow ourselves to have a good belly laugh.

Laughter is beneficial in multiple ways. Physically, laughter stimulates most of the same endorphins (brain chemicals) as exercise and can increase blood flow and energy production. Mentally, laughter helps us to get a nice break from stress and stimulates the relaxation response inside our body and mind. In the 18th century, Sebastian Chamfort wrote, "the most wasted day is one in which we have not laughed."

The famous editor and writer Norman Cousins explained in his best-seller, *Anatomy of an Illness*, how laughter helped him overcome the pain of his severely debilitating disease of the endocrine system. "I made the joyous discovery that ten minutes of genuine belly laughter had an anesthetic effect and would give me at least two hours of pain-free sleep."[4] Part of the therapy he designed for himself included watching Marx Brothers movies and reading humor books.

© Randy Glasbergen.
www.glasbergen.com

"Many people believe that laughter is the best medicine, so the government has declared a ban on all laughing until further studies can be done."

Another great example of mind-body cross training is yoga, which improves the strength, balance, and flexibility of the body while also improving your focus, attention, and mindfulness. Researchers have also begun to evaluate the brain's ability to learn and retain information while the body is engaged in physical activity.

My personal experience is that doing light exercise such as walking on the treadmill or using an elliptical machine helps me focus when I'm trying to do research or be creative. Stimulating circulation increases blood flow, so this may help boost retention, or it might be that having to focus on movement eliminates the brain drain of multiple distractions. When I read on the couch or in my office, my mind wanders. But when I read and walk (which also takes a bit of training, and coordination), I am able to focus on what I'm reading.

Re-directing Our Automatic Pilot – For Good

Building brain endurance requires sustainable habits that support cognitive health and fitness. Being resilient means we are able to sustain the wear and tear of the daily grind. By utilizing the cognitive fitness training program outlined in this book, you can shift your auto-brain away from survival mode and toward a new way of thinking and behaving that moves you in the direction of your goals. It is important to put all the pieces together – the Fab 5 of brain health, training brain strength and flexibility, and developing a realistic program you can stick with.

Most importantly, if we want to train our brain to work more efficiently and to age successfully, we must be as consistent as possible. As we incorporate new supportive habits, we need repetition to continue to make them automated so they require less energy. This kind of frequency keeps us building and maintaining our improved fitness levels.

Have you ever noticed that taking a day off from working out feels great and two feels like a luxury, but after three it's very hard to start again? Vladamir Horowitz, a famous pianist who performed well into his eighties, said this about consistency: "When I miss one day I notice. When I miss two days my wife notices. When I miss three days the world notices."[5]

The most important thing about endurance training is that it supports sustainable behavior change so that you can continue your new brain-healthy lifestyle forever. Remember how important it is to have a supportive story and a purpose that truly matters to you to keep yourself motivated when times get tough. My dear friend Bill McAlpine gave me permission to share a story he uses to help him stay committed to taking care of himself. It's one of my all-time favorites.

"…Because Daddy loves us."

I travel a lot. It is part of the challenge of doing my job. The upside is that when I am home, I am home. Other than the occasional conference call, submitting invoices, and basic office work, my time is mine and I choose to spend as much of it as I can with my wife and two daughters.

But I recognize that in order for me to be the best for my family, I need to first take care of myself. On the surface, taking the time to work out, especially with my heavy work schedule, would appear selfish. In fact, those are the words of a small voice that wells up inside of me. How do you silence that voice and make sure that you take care of the things you know are important, even if that means you need to spend a little more time away from the people who matter the most to you to do so?

If you want to make change, my belief is that you have to change what you believe. You need to change your perception of your situation. If we believe that we are time bankrupt, and that taking care of our self by working out is a selfish act, we will behave accordingly. For me, I needed to change not only my perception of working out, but also the perception of my daughters.

Why do I work out? Do I do it to look better or to feel better? Do I do it just for the pure joy of it? (Hardly!) I found that none of these reasons were meaningful enough to sustain change. It was too easy for me to miss, too superficial of a view for "why." I had to change my perception. I needed to find a core value beyond what marketers, advertisements, or celebrities wanted me to believe mattered.

Why work out? It is an act of love. Never thought of it that way? Me either. But as I thought about my "why" for working out and eating right, I had to figure out what would help me sustain the change. I needed to find a way to make sure that no matter how much I travel, no matter what the circumstances, I would take care of myself.

So I began my indoctrination. I reminded myself of the true reason I do these things – because I love my family. I used this statement as my personal mantra. I shared these thoughts with my family. I began instilling in my daughters at a very young age that the reason why Mommy (my wife is very faithful in her workouts; for me it is an effort) and Daddy work out is because "We love them, and we want to be around for them." My perception changed. My family's perception changed. Taking care of myself stopped being an act of selfishness and became an act of love.

I knew the change stuck when on a warm Central Texas July morning my youngest daughter asked me if I was going to work out today. I was lying on the couch and honestly had no desire to work out. It was hot and I was tired. Missing one day was not a big deal. I'll work out tomorrow, I convinced myself. I turned to my daughter and simply replied, "Naw, I don't think so." I figured that was a good enough answer, and I could go back to more productive activities like watching TV.

My daughter's eyes began to water, and her lower lip started to quiver. She looked at me with her gorgeous brown eyes and said quietly, "Don't you love me?" I felt like someone had just punched me in the gut and knocked all the wind out of me. I stood up and said, "Grab my spandex. I'm riding." The biggest smile came over her and she hugged me, saying, "thank you, Daddy."

The small things really do matter. If you are like me, change may start with shifting your perception of why you do what you do. What do you believe? Simply stated: Anchor change in a core value in order to sustain it.

Action Plan: Sustain Your Brain

You can train your brain to be healthy over time by exercising your endurance, which is a result of using healthy fundamentals and keeping up with your strength and flexibility training. Being consistent with your training program is critical to building sustainability so that you can be healthy and happy and perform at your best over time.

Top Endurance Training Exercises

1. Have More Fun

One of the best ways to improve compliance with any program is to enjoy what you're doing. Many of the experts I consulted for this book suggested finding ways to make training strategies fun so that we are more likely to want to keep doing them, as opposed to feeling like we're punishing ourselves. Exercise is a great example. When we have to drag ourselves out of bed to get to the gym, it often feels like torture – and our brain can easily talk us out of going with a million reasons why it's not such a good idea after all (I need more sleep, I'll get to it later, I'll start again tomorrow, and so on).

Playing sports is a great way to do cross training for the brain and body. Whenever possible, choose sports that challenge your cardiovascular system while also challenging your mind. These activities will increase the strength of your brain cells while also forming more complex connections between them. Not only does that keep you mentally stimulated, but it increases social connection while boosting accountability.

My friend Ron Woods, who worked with the United States Tennis Association for 20 years and now teaches courses at the University of South Florida, has written several books on the benefits of playing sports as we age. He says, "if you're not having fun in physical activity, chances are you're in the wrong sport, workout, or routine and just bored with what used to be fun. You've got to change it up by trying new activities, taking recovery time off, and adding variety to spice up your play."

2. Set SMART goals

It is important that we set goals correctly using the SMART format (specific, measurable, actionable, realistic, and timed). This allows us to be clear on what we are doing, keep track of our progress, and stay confident that the goal is attainable within a certain period of time. Once you start your training program, pay close attention to how you're progressing so that you can make adjustments as needed.

Common mistakes include taking on too many goals at one time, taking on goals that are too lofty, not being specific enough about goals or behaviors, and not being flexible when circumstances change. Life is constantly changing. In order for us to keep with our training program, we need to be willing to adapt. This flexibility allows us to adjust our plan rather than abandon it.

3. Celebrate Small wins

People often get frustrated when they set out on a new training program, follow all of the recommendations, and then see no progress. Many times this lack of momentum is linked to a goal that was too difficult to reach in a realistic period of time. Weight loss is a great example of a training goal that people can quickly give up on when the scale doesn't move fast enough.

Rather than focus on the outcome, it may be helpful to break the goal down into smaller goals so that you can see the progress you're making and stop to celebrate your success along the way. It's easy to move right from one goal to the next and forget that establishing the first set of habits was a big deal. Having small wins along the way helps us see progress and stay motivated.

4. Build Accountability

A key to consistency is holding yourself accountable. But often that's not enough. By using a training log regularly, you are accountable to yourself; however, it's easy to give ourselves excuses as to why we're not getting things done. Try telling someone else the same "story" we use to convince ourselves we need to sleep in longer, clean our plate, or skip a social gathering.

Making your goal known to others helps make it more real and gives us someone to follow up with. Determine how you will check in (email, phone, in person) and when (every day, every Friday, at staff meetings), then build in rewards if you think they will be helpful for you (lunch, massage, vacation day).

5. Do Some Good

According to Dr. Seligman and his colleagues at the University of Pennsylvania, doing something kind for someone else produces the single most reliable momentary increase in well-being.[6] Of all the positive-psychology strategies tested by his team, doing a gratitude visit produced the largest positive changes in happiness, and the positive effects lasted for a month.

A great way to boost positivity while adding a stronger sense of purpose to your training program is to get involved with a charity you believe in. There are many ways to get involved, and many causes that would love your support. By signing up for a training program or event that also helps someone else, you boost your positivity and sense of purpose and increase social connections, all while training your brain and your body.

The following charities have fund-raising events you can participate in, or training programs that help you prepare for an endurance event such as a half marathon, full marathon, or triathlon (just to name a few). This particular list includes groups that the *SYNERGY* team has personally been involved with. It's not all inclusive. However, we are constantly updating our list of "do good groups" on our website, so please email me at coach@synergyprograms.com if you would like to add a favorite charity to the list.

- Alzheimer's Association – www.alz.org
- Team in Training (Leukemia & Lymphoma Society) – www.teamintraining.org
- Livestrong – www.livestrong.org
- Challenged Athletes Foundation – www.challengedathletes.org
- American Diabetes Association – www.diabetes.org
- Girls on the Run – www.girlsontherun.org

- Team for Kids – www.nyrrf.org
- Wounded Warrior Foundation – www.warriorfoundation.com
- Special Operations Warrior Foundation – www.specialops.org

Recap Top Techniques for Endurance Training:

1. Have more fun
2. Set SMART goals
3. Celebrate small wins
4. Build accountability
5. Do some good

SHARP Sprints

The following are quick activities that support mental endurance:

• *Write down your purpose*

Answer the following questions: "My purpose in life is…" and then "My purpose for today is…"

• *Do an Intentional Act of Kindness*

Create a ritual to do one nice thing for someone your know, or don't know, every day. Plan it out and track it, in order to establish a new habit.

• *Add accountability*

It is much easier to talk yourself out of doing something than to justify it to someone else. Our "story" may work for us but sound silly to our friend, family member, or colleague. Use this to your advantage by adding as much accountability to your training program as possible.

• *Treat yourself*

Non-caloric treats are a fun way to make sure your motivation stays fired up without packing on the pounds or causing a sugar-induced energy roller coaster. Examples might be a new pair of jeans, a massage, new music, or even just scheduling an extra break each day for a week to go for a relaxing walk.

- *Cross train*

Activities like journaling, meditation, visualization, biofeedback, skills-based physical activity, socializing around hobbies, and playing sports provide benefit in multiple dimensions – body, mind, and spirit. By cross-training, your consistency may improve because you get a greater return on your time and energy investment.

Training Take Away: To build resilience we must have a *consistent* program that we can use on a *regular basis* and that we will be able to *maintain over time*. Remember, we're doing more than just adding years to our life – we're adding life to our years. Training our brain to be stronger and more *resilient* is *endurance training* for the brain, which allows us to bring our best mental energy to the present moment and for many years to come.

(Find more exercises in the resources section)

PART THREE – CREATE YOUR PLAN

In order to develop a *SHARP* brain, we need to create a plan that will maximize your return on investment. To do that, it is important to utilize training principles that will work effectively, and then follow the *SHARP* Strategies to keep your training consistent and sustainable.

STEP SEVEN
Design your cognitive fitness training program

Three Key Principles of Brain Training
When choosing exercises to help train your brain, keep in mind the following principles for improving fitness, (based on the American College of Sports Medicine's physical fitness guidelines), which also apply to improving the fitness of your brain.

1. It must be specific – You wouldn't work out your bicep and expect to get bigger calves. If you want to be more focused, do focusing exercises. To have a more optimistic outlook, do positivity training.

2. It must be challenging – If you do something the way you've always done it, your brain (or body) doesn't have to work at it. In order to stimulate growth, it's important to do exercises and activities that cause a bit of discomfort. Then you'll stimulate the adaptation process that will lead to improvements.

Playing cards or doing crossword puzzles can be considered mental strength training when they are challenging. But if you've become a master card player (like my dad, who was able to play cards while driving to softball tournaments, which is not a training strategy I'd recommend), then you are pretty much playing with your auto-brain and will not see any cognitive benefits.

3. It must be practiced consistently – Remember, just like the muscles in our body, the brain follows a "use it or lose it" philosophy, as we discussed in the section on brain basics. Experts have long said that when it comes to the brain, "what fires together, wires together" and "what fires apart, wires apart." In order to maintain your previous gains and continue to see improvements, it is important to be consistent with your training program.

SHARP Strategies to Make Training Stick

I promised myself I would never use a "cheesy" acronym in one of my books, but I couldn't help myself with this one. Believe it or not, I was actually working on suggestions for maintaining positive behavior change and started to see the letters *S-H-A-R-P* coming together right before my eyes, so I guess it was "meant to be."

To stay sharp, it's important to have a plan that provides structure for the journey ahead. When designing your plan, keep the following concepts in mind:

S – Simple strategy: It can feel overwhelming to think of all the things we could do to have a healthier, more "fit" brain. Be sure to keep your strategies simple so that it's realistic for you to incorporate them into your busy schedule.

H – Helpful tools: There are a lot of tools available to facilitate your training, which can be helpful along the way by providing guidance, support, and accountability. For some recommended online tools for brain training, see the resources section.

A – Accountability: One of the best ways to increase compliance with any training program is to build in accountability with yourself and ideally with other people you care about. Using a training log to track your progress will help you stay accountable. Sharing the log with someone else will boost your level of commitment because it's harder to slack off when someone else is monitoring your progress. Talking about what you're working on makes it feel more real, and reminds us that people are going to be watching how we follow through.

R – *Routine*: As much as possible, use strategies that you can incorporate into your current routine. For example, if you want to remember to take your vitamins, set them out by your coffee pot since your auto-brain is already driving you in that direction in the morning. Or if you want to remind yourself of a positive mantra you've created, write it on a Post-it Note and put it on your computer. Take this a step further by rewriting your mantra every morning to increase mental stimulation and solidify new brain connections.

P – *Practice*: Any new behavior is going to take an investment of time and energy in order to make it a habit, so design your training plan using the previous suggestions and then practice, practice, practice. When things don't change as quickly as you might like, remind yourself that you're working on re-wiring a system that's been pretty well established by old habits, and don't be too hard on yourself. Schedule practice time into your day and make it a priority, and in time you will see results.

Wrapping It Up

As you begin your *SHARP* training program, I want to encourage you to create a plan that will help you perform at your best, build resilience, and maintain good brain health and functioning over time. If you have not already done so, revisit the brain health assessment in Part One to help you determine which area you should focus on first. As you begin to select strategies to use, consider your strength, flexibility, and endurance goals. Finally, create a training plan that is specific, challenging, and practiced consistently. I recommend that you come up with one brain health and one brain fitness strategy to start with, and then as you make progress you can add more to your plan.

Keep in mind that every journey begins with that first step, and you've already done that by investigating ways to keep yourself sharp. My friend, Admiral Ray Smith, continues to remind me that it's the little things that make a difference in accomplishing the big things. "These habits, along with a multitude of others, contribute to your self-image, your marriage, your family, and ultimately the fullness of your life," he told me. "Having said this, I recognize how difficult this is. That is why all of us need to focus on an orderly and consistent program of developing habits. As we say in the SEALs, 'The only easy day was yesterday.' "

You've taken the first step – now be focused, flexible, and consistent, and keep your brain *SHARP* to enjoy a healthy, happy, and successful life for a long time to come.

CONCLUSION

My Story

Most authors start a book like this one with a personal story or an explanation of what makes them an expert on the topic. But I've decided to save that part for last because this book is not about me. It's about you. And I want to make that very clear. However, something I've learned over the last decade of coaching, speaking, and traveling is that we all learn from each other, and having authentic conversations is an important part of making a connection that takes this message from being a lecture to a partnership. So I would like to share a bit about my story, my goals, and why this book is an important part of my personal life mission.

Goal #1: A stronger brain to take me where I never thought I could go – Strength training. As I have mentioned, mental strength training has enabled me to be able to face two of my biggest fears on a regular basis: flying and public speaking (the third is medical doctors due to some challenges I had early on in my life, so when I have to travel on a plane to speak to physicians, it's about as challenging as it gets). In fact, when I first took this job as a performance coach and trainer, I told my interviewer that I had absolutely no interest in ever traveling for work or getting up on a stage. No way.

Up to that point, the only way I could persuade myself to get on an airplane was when I had to travel to visit my family or keep my softball scholarship in college (and I continued to be a "white knuckle" traveler the whole time). I had to change my mindset to think differently in order to be able to continue a professional journey that I was grateful for and proud of. I consistently practice these strategies to continue on this path because I feel a strong connection to the purpose of what I am doing.

Goal #2: Figuring out how to be more resilient to stress – Flexibility training. Resilience became a critical factor in keeping my professional journey moving forward when I suddenly found myself in the hospital twice in one week for unknown reasons. The level of anxiety I was experiencing with the traveling and speaking was so intense that when I became injured and couldn't exercise, the toxic stress hormones became overwhelming and my system just quit. I became physically exhausted and experienced severe anxiety that lasted for two weeks, without a moment's rest. At that point I decided I had to quit my job because there was no other solution.

Fortunately, friends and family rallied around me and reminded me that I was stronger than I thought, and that I had been given an amazing opportunity that I couldn't give up without a good fight. Six years, hundreds of presentations, and over a dozen international trips later, I still get sweaty palms sometimes. I still have an energy crash from time to time, and find myself getting out of balance. But maintaining self-care rituals, balancing stress and recovery, and keeping up with consistent nutrition and exercise practices are no longer optional. They have become part of my job description, and the job description of the members of my team (a monthly massage – or other spa service – is mandatory and paid for by the company).

Goal #3: Healthy aging – Endurance training. I had another shock to my system when I first experienced losing a loved one to Alzheimer's disease. I had always been interested in brain health and performance, but it wasn't until I spent time with my grandmother that I fully realized the magnitude of what brain disease (or injury) can rob from us.

Of all the possible illnesses, brain disease not only changes your body but it changes your soul. As the mind deteriorates, personality changes drastically, and someone who was once sweet, loving, and kind can become angry, irritable, and mean. (Thankfully, I did not experience this with any of my family members, but I have witnessed it in other Alzheimer's patients and heard horrible stories from caregivers).

Impulse control goes away, and bizarre behaviors start to manifest. Caregiving quickly becomes a 24/7 job, usually taken on by loved ones who despite all the best intentions don't always know where to reach out for help. Around that time I was working in Australia and happened to pick up a book simply because I liked the cover and it was recommended on a list of staff favorites. "Still Alice" is one of the best books I have read, but also one of the most disturbing. It completely changed my perspective on what it would be like to suffer from a brain disease like Alzheimer's.[1]

For someone who invests a great amount in self-improvement and education, the thought of suddenly losing my sense of self really shook me up. I immediately contacted my local Alzheimer's Association chapter and volunteered to help promote awareness and prevention efforts, which is part of my personal mission in writing this book. (A portion of the proceeds from this book are being donated to the Alzheimer's Association – www.alz.org.)

While there is still no treatment for Alzheimer's disease and other forms of dementia, studies consistently show that we can prevent or at least delay the development of these diseases through the brain health and fitness strategies discussed in this book. I call this my "sneak attack" to making people healthier.

Focus on your performance, resilience, and longevity at work and you will find yourself living a healthier, happier life by accident. What a wonderful side effect!

Wishing you all the health, happiness, and success in life you can possibly stand. HH

If I Had My Life to Live Over
by Nadine Stair (at age 85)

I'd dare to make more mistakes next time.
I'd relax. I would limber up.
I would be sillier than I have been this trip.
I would take fewer things seriously.
 I would take more chances.
     I would climb more mountains and swim more rivers.
I would eat more ice cream and less beans.
I would perhaps have more actual troubles
but I'd have fewer imaginary ones.
     You see, I'm one of those people who live
sensibly and sanely hour after hour,
day after day.
     Oh, I've had my moments,
and if I had it to do over again,
 I'd have more of them.
In fact, I'd try to have nothing else.
 Just moments, one after another,
instead of living so many years ahead of each day.
     I've been one of those people who never go anywhere
without a thermometer, a hot water bottle, a raincoat
and a parachute.
If I had to do it again, I would travel lighter than I have.
     If I had my life to live over,
I would start barefoot earlier in the spring
and stay that way later in the fall.
I would go to more dances.
I would ride more merry-go-rounds.
I would pick more daisies.

REFERENCES

Introduction

1) Hanson, R., (2009). *Buddha's Brain: The Practical Neuroscience of Happiness, Love, and Wisdom.* Oakland, CA: New Harbinger Publications.

2) Adams, J., (2009). Cost Savings from Health Promotion and Stress Management Interventions. *OD Practitioner, 41 (4),* 31-37.

3) Families and Work Institute, (2008). The State of Health in the American Workforce: Does having an effective workplace matter? Retrieved from www.familiesandwork.org

4) Alzheimer's Association, (2010). 2010 Alzheimer's disease Facts and Figures. Retrieved from http://www.alz.org/documents_custom/report_alzfactsfigures2010.pdf

5) Snowdon, D., (1997). Aging and Alzheimer's Disease: Lessons From the Nun Study. *The Gerontologist, 37 (2),* 150-156.

6) Buettner, D., (2008). *The Blue Zones: Lessons for Living Longer From the People Who've Lived the Longest.* Washington, DC: National Geographic Books.

PART ONE
Step Two - Understand Brain Basics
1) Doidge, N., (2007). *The Brain That Changes Itself: Stories of Personal Triumph from the Frontiers of Brain Science.* New York, NY: The Penguin Group.

2) Begley, S., (2007). *Train Your Mind, Change Your Brain: How a New Science Reveals Our Extraordinary Potential to Transform Ourselves.* New York, NY: Ballantine Books.

3) Medina, J., (2009). *Brain Rules.* Seattle, WA: Pear Press.

4) Ratey, J., with Hagerman, E., (2008). *Spark: the revolutionary science of exercise and the brain.* New York, NY: Little, Brown and Company.

5) Loehr, J., and Schwartz, T., (2003). *The Power of Full Engagement: Managing Energy, Not Time, is the Key to High Performance and Personal Renewal.* New York, NY: Free Press.

Rule #1 - Food is Fuel
1) Fernandez, A., and Goldberg, E., (2009). *The Guide to Brain Fitness: 18 interviews with scientists, practical advice, and product reviews, to keep your brain sharp.* Retrieved from http://www.sharpbrains.com/book/

2) Buettner, D., (2008). *The Blue Zones: Lessons for Living Longer From the People Who've Lived the Longest.* Washington, DC: National Geographic Books.

3) Williams, J., Plassman, B., Burke, J., Holsinger, T., Benjamin S., (April 2010). Preventing Alzheimer's Disease and Cognitive Decline. Evidence Report/Technology Assessment No. 193. Rockville, MD: Agency for Healthcare Research and Quality.

4) Scarmeas, N., et al. (August 2009) Physical Activity, Diet, and risk of Alzheimer disease. *JAMA, 302(6),* 627-37.

5) American Heart Association, (2002). Fish Consumption, Fish Oil, Omega-3 Fatty Acids, and Cardiovascular Disease. *Circulation, 106,* 2747-2757.

6) Buell, J., Scott, T., Dawson-Hughes, B., Dallal, G., Rosenberg, I., Folstein, M., and Tucker, K., (2009). Vitamin D Is Associated With Cognitive Function in Elders Receiving Home Health Services. *J Gerontol A Biol Sci Med Sci, 64A (8),* 888-895.

7) Holick, M., (2007). Vitamin D Deficiency. *N Engl J Med, 357 (3),* 266-281.

8) American Dietetic Association, (2010). Press Release: American Dietetic Association Supports New Institute of Medicine Recommendations on Calcium and Vitamin D Intake. Retrieved from: http://www.eatright.org/Media/content.aspx?i

d=6442460107&terms=guidelines+vitamin+D
+

9) Slutsky, I., et al, (2010). Enhancement of Learning and Memory by Elevating Brain Magnesium. Neron, 65 (2), 165-177.

10) Snowdon,D., Tully, C., Smith, C., Perez Riley, K., and Markesbery, W., (2007). Serum folate and the severity of atrophy of the neocortex in Alzheimer disease: findings from the Nun Study. *Am J Clin Nutr, 71,* 993–998.

11) Consumer Reports, (2010). Multivitamins: Most we tested were fine, so select by price. Retrieved from http://www.consumerreports.org/health/natur al-health/multivitamins/overview/index.htm

12) Restak, R., (2009). *Think Smart: A Neuroscientist's Prescription for Improving Your Brain's Performance.* New York, NY: Riverhead Books.

13) Lopez, O., Becker, J., Kuller, L., Ho, A., Parikshak, N., Hua, X., Leow, A., and Toga, A., (2009). Obesity Bad for the Brain: Mapping Study Suggests Brain Shrinkage in Obese Elderly Could Increase Alzheimer's Risk.

14) Raji, C., et al, (2010). Brain Structure and Obesity. *Hum Brain Mapp, 31(3),* 353-364.

15) Xu, W., Atti, A., Gatz, , M., Pedersen, N., Johnson, B., and Fratiglioni, L., (2011). Midlife overweight and obesity increase late-life dementia risk: A population-based twin study. *Neurology, 76 (18),* 1568-1574.

16) Gardner, C., Kiazand, A., Alhassan, S., Kim, S., Stafford, R., Balise, R., Kraemer, H., King, A., (2007). Comparison of the Atkins, Zone, Ornish, and LEARN Diets for Change in Weight and Related Risk Factors Among Overweight Premenopausal Women: The A TO Z Weight Loss Study: A Randomized Trial. *JAMA, 297(9),* 969-977.

17) Amen, D., (2010). *Change Your Brain, Change Your Body: Use Your Brain to Get and Keep the Body You Have Always Wanted.* New York, NY: Three Rivers Press.

Rule #2 - Activity is Activating

1) Medina, J., (2009). *Brain Rules.* Seattle, WA: Pear Press.

2) Katzmarzyk, P., Church, T., Craig, C., and Bouchard, C., (2009). Sitting Time and Mortality from All Causes, Cardiovascular Disease, and Cancer. *Med. Sci. Sports Exerc, 41 (5),* 998–1005.

3) Levine, J., (2010). Your Chair: Comfortable but Deadly. *Diabetes, 59, (11),* 2715-2716.

4) Colcombe, S., Kramer, A., Erickson, K., Scalf, P., McAuley, E., Cohen, N., Webb, A., Jerome,

G., Marquez, D., and Elavsky, S., (2004).
Cardiovascular fitness, cortical plasticity, and
aging. *PNAS, 101(9),* 3316-3321.

5) Ratey, J., with Hagerman, E., (2008). *Spark: the
revolutionary science of exercise and the brain.* New
York, NY: Little, Brown and Company.

6) Colcombe, S., Erickson, K., Scalf, P., Kim, J.,
Prakash, R., (2006). Exercise: An Active Route
to Healthy Aging Aerobic Exercise Training
Increases Brain Volume in Aging Humans.
Journal of Gerontology: Medical Sciences, 61A (11),
1166–1170.

7) Yaffe, K., Barnes, D., Nevitt, M., Lui, L., and
Covinsky, K., (2001). A Prospective Study of
Physical Activity and Cognitive Decline in
Elderly Women: Women Who Walk. *Arch Intern
Med, 161,* 1703-1708.

8) Steyn, N., (2004). Diet, nutrition and the
prevention of type 2 diabetes. *Public Health
Nutrition, 7(1A),* 147–165.

9) Public Broadcasting System, (2008). Depression
Fact Sheet. Retrieved from
http://www.pbs.org/wgbh/takeonestep/depres
sion/resources.html

10) Blumenthal, J., et al, (2007) Exercise and
Pharmacotherapy in the Treatment of Major
Depressive Disorder. *Psychosomatic Medicine, 69,*
587–596.

172

11) Haskell, W., et al, (2007). Physical Activity and Public Health: Updated Recommendation for Adults from the American College of Sports Medicine and the American Heart Association. *Med Sci Sports Exerc, 39, (8),* 1423–1434.

12) Tanasescu, M., (2002). Exercise type and intensity in relation to coronary heart disease in men. *JAMA; 288(16),* 1994–2000.

13) Achor, S., (2010). *The Happiness Advantage: The Seven Principals of Positive Psychology That Fuel Success and Performance at Work.* New York, NY: Crown Business.

Rule #3 - Balancing Stress Balances Life

1) Ratey, J., with Hagerman, E., (2008). *Spark: the revolutionary science of exercise and the brain.* New York, NY: Little, Brown and Company.

2) Sapolsky, R., (2004). *Why Zebras Don't Get Ulcers (3rd Edition).* New York, NY: Holt Paperbacks.

3) *Golf Digest,* (Oct 2010). How to Train Your Brain: Good thinking might beat out a good stroke. Retrieved from http://www.golfdigest.com/golf-instruction/short-game/putting/2010-10/putting-guy-yocom-brain?currentPage=2

4) Talbott, S., (2002). *The Cortisol Connection: Why Stress Makes You Fat and Ruins Your Health - and*

What You Can Do About It. Alameda, CA: Hunter House.

5) Epel, E., Lapidus, R., McEwen, B., Brownell, K., (2001). Stress may add bite to appetite in women: a laboratory study of stress-induced cortisol and eating behavior. *Psychoneuroendocrinology 26,* 37-49.

6) Groppel, J., (1999). *The Corporate Athlete: How to Achieve Maximal Performance in Business and Life.* Somerset, NJ: Wiley.

7) Ariga, A., and Lleras, A., (2011). Brief and rare mental "breaks" keep you focused: Deactivation and reactivation of task goals preempt vigilance decrements. *Cognition, 118 (3),* 439-443.

Rule #4 - Resting Is Working

1) The Better Sleep Council, (2007). Position Statement: Poor Sleep Affecting Accuracy And Attitude On The Job New National Better Sleep Month Survey Highlights Link between Sleep and Work Performance. Retrieved from http://www.bettersleep.org/Pressroom/press-release.aspx?id=4

2) Ferrie, J., et al, (2011). Change in sleep duration and cognitive function: findings from the Whitehall II study. *Sleep, 34 (5),* 565-573.

3) Maas, J., (1998). *Power Sleep: The Revolutionary Program That Prepares Your Mind for Peak Performance.* New York, NY: Harper Paperbacks.

4) Diekelmann, S., Büchel, C., Born, J., Björn, R., (2011). Labile or stable: opposing consequences for memory when reactivated during waking and sleep. *Nature Neuroscience, 14,* 381–386.

5) Basner, M., Dinges, D., (2011). Maximizing sensitivity of the psychomotor vigilance test (PVT) to sleep loss. *Sleep, 34(5),* 581-591.

6) National Center for Health Statistics, (2008). Sleep Duration as a Correlate of Smoking, Alcohol Use, Leisure-Time Physical Inactivity, and Obesity Among Adults: United States, 2004-200. Retrieved from http://www.cdc.gov/nchs/data/hestat/sleep04-06/sleep04-06.htm

Rule #5 - A Social Life is Life Support

1) Holt-Lunstad J., Smith T., Layton J., (2010). Social Relationships and Mortality Risk: A Meta-analytic Review. *Plos Med, 7(7),* 1-20.

2) Vaillant, G., (2009). Yes, I stand by my words, Happiness equals love- full stop. Retrieved on January 26, 2011 from: www.positivepsychologynews.com

3) Cacioppo, J. and Patrick, W., (2008). *Loneliness: Human Nature and the Need for Social Connection.* New York, NY: W.W. Norton & Company.

4) Reis, H., and Gable, S., (2003). Toward a Positive Psychology of Relationships. In Keyes,

C., and Haidt, J., (2003). *Flourishing: Positive Psychology and the Life Well-Lived*. Washington, DC: American Psychological Association.

5) Klepeis, N., Nelson, W., Ott, W., et al, (2001). The National Human Activity Pattern Survey (NHAPS): A resource for assessing exposure to environmental pollutants. *J Exposure Analysis and Environmental Epidemiology, 11,* 231-252.

6) Ybarra, O., Bernstein, E., Winkielman, P., Keller, M., Manis, M., Chan, E., and Rodriguez, J., (2008). Mental Exercising Through Simple Socializing: Social Interaction Promotes General Cognitive Functioning. *PSPB, 34 (2),* 248-259.

7) Hawkley, L. Masi, M., Berry, D., and Cacioppo, T., (2006). Loneliness is a unique predictor of age-related differences in systolic blood pressure. *Psychology and Aging 21(1),* 152 – 164.

8) Berkman, L., Leo-Summers, L., Horwitz, R., (1992). Emotional Support and Survival after Myocardial Infarction: A Prospective, Population-based Study of the Elderly. *Ann Intern Med, 117, (12),* 1003-1009.

9) Bloom, J., (2001). Sources of support and the physical and mental well-being of young women with breast cancer. *Social Science & Medicine, 53 (11),* 1513-1524.

10) Schnall, S., Harber, K., Stefanucci, J., Proffitt, D., (2008). Social support and the perception of geographical slant. *Journal of Experimental Social Psychology, 44,* 1246–1255.

11) Rath, T., and Harter, J., (2010). *Wellbeing: The Five Essential Elements.* Washington, DC: Gallup Press.

STEP FOUR
Build Mental Muscle (strength training)

1) Dean, D. & Webb, C., (Jan 2011). Recovering from information overload: Always-on, multitasking work environments are killing productivity, dampening creativity, and making us unhappy. Retrieved from http://www.mckinseyquarterly.com/Recovering_from_information_overload_2735

2) Asplund, C., Dux, P., Ivanoff, J., and Marois, R., (2006). Isolation of a central bottleneck of information processing with time-resolved fMRI. *Neuron, 52, (6),* 1109–1120.

3) Aral, S., Brynjolfsson, E., Van Alstyne, M., (2007). Information Technology and Information, Worker Productivity: Task Level Evidence. Retrieved from http://digital.mit.edu/research/papers/info_technology_278.pdf

4) Shellenbarger, S., (Feb 2003). Wall Street Journal: Multitasking Makes You Stupid: Studies Show Pitfalls of Doing Too Much at Once.

Retrieved from
https://www.wallstreetjournal.com

5) Seigel, D., (2010). *Mindsight: The New Science of Transformation*. New York, NY: Random House.
6) Gallagher, W., (2009). *Rapt: Attention and the Focused Life*. New York, NY: Penguin Press.

7) Ariga, A., and Lleras, A., (2011). Brief and rare mental 'breaks' keep you focused: Deactivation and reactivation of task goals preempt vigilance decrements. *Cognition, 118, (3),* 439-443.

8) González , V., and Mark, G., (2004). Constant, Constant, Multi-tasking Craziness": Managing Multiple Working Spheres. *CHI04, 6 (1).*

9) Gallup Management Journal, (2006). Too Many Interruptions at Work? Retrieved from http://gmj.gallup.com/content/23146/too-many-interruptions-work.aspx

10) Allen, D., (2002). *Getting Things Done: The Art of Stress-Free Productivity*. New York, NY: Penguin.

11) Drucker, P., (1967). *The Effective Executive*. New York, NY: HarperCollins Publisher.

12) Cilley, M., (2002). *Sink Reflections*. New York, NY: Bantam Books.

STEP FIVE
Develop Resilience (flexibility training)

1) Levy, B., et al, (2002). Longevity increased by positive self-perceptions of aging. *Journal of Personality and Social Psychology, 83(2),* 261-270.

2) Langer, E., (2009). *Counterclockwise: Mindful Health and the Power of Possibility.* New York, NY: Ballantine Books.

3) Loehr, J., (2007). *The Power of Story.* New York, NY: Simon & Schuster Inc.

4) Margolis, M., (2009). *Believe Me: Why Your Vision, Brand, and Leadership Need a Bigger Story.* Retrieved from www.believemethebook.com

5) Dweck, C. (2006). Mindset: *The New Psychology of Success.* New York, NY: Random House.

6) Fredrickson, B., (2009). *Positivity: Groundbreaking Research Reveals How to Embrace the Hidden Strength of Positive Emotions, Overcome Negativity, and Thrive.* New York, NY: Crown Archetype.

7) Fredrickson, B. and Branigan, C., (2005). Positive emotions broaden the scope of attention and thought-action repertoires. *Cognition and Emotion,* 19, 313-332.

8) Fredrickson, B., Tugade, M., Waugh, E., & Larkin, G. (2003). What good are positive emotions in crises?: A prospective study of resilience and emotions following the terrorist

attacks on the United States on September 11th, 2001. *Journal of Personality and Social Psychology, 84*, 365-376.

9) Fredrickson, B., & Joiner, T. (2002). Positive emotions trigger upward spirals toward emotional well-being. *Psychological Science, 13*, 172-175.

10) Steptoe, A., Wardle, J., and Marmot, M., (2005). Positive affect and health-related neuroendocrine, cardiovascular, and inflammatory processes. *PNAS, 102 (18),* 6508-6512.

11) Gil, K., Carson, J., Porter, L., Scipio, C., Bediako, S., & Orringer, E., (2004). Daily mood and stress predict pain, health care use, and work activity in African American adults with sickle-cell disease. *Health Psychology, 23,* 267–274.

12) Ostir, G., Markides, K., Peek, K., & Goodwin, J., (2001). The Association Between Emotional Well-Being and the Incidence of Stroke in Older Adults. *Psychosomatic Medicine, 63 (2),* 210-215.

13) Syme, S., & Balfour, J., (1997). Explaining inequalities in coronary heart disease. *The Lancet, 350,* 231-232.

14) Kessler, D. (2009). *The End of Overeating: Taking Control of the Insatiable American Appetite.* Emmaus, PA: Rodale Press, Inc.

15) Lyubomirsky, S. (2008). *The how of happiness: A scientific approach to getting the life you want.* New York: Penguin Press.

16) Lyubomirsky, S., King, L., and Diener, E., (2005). The Benefits of Frequent Positive Affect: Does Happiness Lead to Success? *Psychological Bulletin, 131(6),* 803-855.

17) Crum, A. and Langer, E., (2007). Mind-set matters: exercise and the placebo effect. *Psychol Sci, 18 (2),* 165-171.

18) Karl, K., O'Leary-Kelly, A., and Martocchio, L., (1993). The impact of feedback and self-efficacy on performance in training. *Journal of Organizational Behavior, 14 (4),* 379–394.

19) Fredrickson, B., and Losada, M., (2005). Positive Affect and the Complex Dynamics of Human Flourishing. *American Psychologist, 60,* 678- 686.

20) Gottman, J., (1995). *Why Marriages Succeed or Fail: And How You Can Make Yours Last.* New York, NY: Simon & Schuster.

21) Seligman, M., Steen, T., Park, N., & Peterson, C., (2005). Positive psychology progress: Empirical validation of interventions. *American Psychologist, 60,* 410-421.

22) Emmons, R., McCullough, M., (2003). Counting Blessings Versus Burdens: An Experimental Investigation of Gratitude and Subjective Well-Being in Daily Life. *Journal of Personality, 84 (2),* 377–389.

23) Bolte, A., et al, (2003). Emotion and Intuition: Effects of Positive and negative Mood on Implicit Judgments of Semantic Coherence. *Psychological Science, 14,* 416-421.

STEP SIX
Make it Last (endurance training)

1) Gallagher, W., (2009). *Rapt: Attention and the Focused Life.* New York, NY: Penguin Press.

2) Leider, R., (1997). *The Power of Purpose: Creating Meaning in Your Life and Work.* San Francisco, CA: Berrett-Koehler Publishers.

3) Xu, W., Qui, C., Gatz, M., et al., (2009). Mid- and late-life diabetes in relation to the risk of dementia: a population-based twin study. *Diabetes, 58(1),* 71-77.

4) Cousins, N., (2001). *Anatomy of an Illness as Perceived by the Patient: Reflections on Healing and Regeneration.* New York, NY: W. W. Norton & Company.

5) Coyle, D. (2009). *The Talent Code.* New York, NY: Bantam Books.

6) Seligmen, M., Steen, T., Park, N. and Peterson, C., (2005). Positive Psychology Progress: Empirical Validation of Interventions. *American Psychologist, 60,* 410- 421.

Conclusion
1) Genova, L., (2007). *Still Alice.* Bloomington, IN: iUniverse, Inc.

RESOURCES

Recommended Reading List

STEP ONE – Assessments
VIA Values In Action – Measures optimism through character strengths. Developed and provided online by Martin Seligman, University of Pennsylvania, at: www.authentichappiness.org.

Positivity Ratio self-test, provided online by Barbara Fredrickson at http://www.positivityratio.com/single.php

STEP TWO – Brain Basics
Brain Rules, John Medina, PhD

Change Your Brain, Change Your Body, Daniel Amen, MD

Mindsight, Dan Seigel, MD

The Brain that Changes Itself, Norman Doidge, MD

The Owner's Manual for the Brain, Pierce Howard, PhD

The Talent Code, Daniel Coyle

Train Your Mind, Change Your Brain, Sharon Begley

STEP THREE – Brain Health
General Brain Health
The Dana Guide to Brain Health, by Floyd Bloom, MD, M. Flint Beal, MD, & David Kupfer, MD

Nutrition
You On a Diet: The Owner's Manual for Weight Management, Michael Roizen, MD & Mehmet Oz, MD

Exercise
SPARK: The Revolutionary New Science of Exercise and the Brain, John Ratey, MD

Stress Management
Why Zebras Get Ulcers, Robert Sapolsky, PhD

Sleep
Power Sleep, The Revolutionary Program that Prepares Your Mind for Peak Performance, James Maas, PhD

National Sleep Foundation Website -
www.nationalsleepfoundation.org

*Your Guide to Healthy Sleep,*National Institutes of Health
http://www.nhlbi.nih.gov/health/public/sleep/

Social Connection
Loneliness: Human Nature and the Need for Connection,
John Cacioppo, PhD & William Patrick

STEP FOUR – Strength Training
A Sheep Falls Out of the Tree: And Other Techniques to Develop an Incredible Memory and Boost Brainpower, Christiane Stenger, World Memory Champion

Counterclockwise: Mindful Health and the Power of Possibility, Ellen Langer, PhD

Getting Things Done: The Art of Stress-Free Productivity, David Allen

Rapt: Attention and the Focused Life, Winifred Gallagher

Moonwalking with Einstein: The Art and Science of Remembering Everything, Joshua Foer

Think Smart: A Neuroscientists Prescription for Improving Your Brain's Performance, Richard Restak, MD

STEP FIVE – Flexibility Training
Authentic Happiness: Using the New Positive Psychology to Realize Your Potential for Lasting Fulfillment, Martin Seligman, PhD

Mindset: The New Psychology of Success – Carol Dweck, PhD

The Happiness Advantage: The Seven Principles of Positive Psychology That Fuel Success and Performance at Work, Shawn Achor

The Relaxation Response, Herbert Benson, MD & Miriam Z. Klipper

STEP SIX– Endurance Training

The Anti-Alzheimer's Prescription: The Science-Proven Plan to Start at Any Age, Vincent Fortanasce, MD

The Blue Zones: Lessons for Living Longer From the People Who've Lived the Longest, Dan Buettner

The Harvard Medical School Guide to Achieving Optimal Memory, Aaron P. Nelson, PhD

The Power of Purpose: Creating Meaning in Your Life and Work, Richard J Leider

Training Toolbox
SYNERGY Fab 5 Key Strategies

Nutrition - The five key elements of a brain healthy diet are:

1. Manage glucose levels by eating light, often and balanced
2. Enjoy foods with high nutrient value the majority of the time (especially fruits, vegetables, and omega-3 fatty acids)
3. Limit brain drainers by eating real food whenever possible
4. Keep blood flow running smoothly (decrease blood fat and inflammation)
5. Maintain a healthy weight

Physical Activity - To optimize circulation and physical energy through activity:

1. Look for opportunities to add movement to your day
2. Never sit for longer than 90 minutes at a time
3. Exercise aerobically at least 3x a week
4. Perform strength training exercises at least 2x a week
5. Decrease activation energy

Stress Management – To keep stress levels balanced with relaxation:

1. Stress is necessary
2. Recovery is not an option
3. Oscillating is optimal
4. Practice makes relaxation easier
5. Self-care must be scheduled

Sleep – To repair and rebuild the body and the mind:

1. We work while we sleep
2. Sleep is also critical for repairing and rebuilding
3. Most people require 6-8 hours of sleep
4. Breaks during the day help facilitate healthy oscillation
5. Bed time rituals induce optimal sleep

Tips:
- Go to bed early
- If you have trouble falling asleep, get out of bed and do something relaxing.
- If you take a nap, keep it brief. Nap for less than an hour and before 3 p.m.
- Go to bed and wake up at consistent times, even on weekends.
- Avoid caffeine in the afternoon and at night.
- Dim the lights in the evening
- Let in the sunlight in the morning to boost your alertness.
- Take some time to "wind down" before going to bed.
- Avoid stimulating activities such as TV, phone, and computer.
- Never eat a large meal right before bedtime.
- Enjoy a healthy snack or light dessert so you don't go to bed hungry.

Social Connection – To provide social support and a sense of belonging:

1. Isolation can be bad for your health
2. Social connection is based on perception
3. Being alone doesn't have to be lonely
4. Schedule social engagements
5. Cross train with social activities that boost health

More on the Mediterranean Diet

Sample Mediterranean Diet Inspired Meals Options
Breakfast:
Omelet with as many fresh veggies as you enjoy. Add lean turkey, chicken, beans, and salsa if you like them.
Whole grain toast with peanut butter.
Oatmeal with cinnamon, chopped walnuts, and blueberries.

Lunch:
Salad with lean protein such as fish, chicken, chickpeas, beans, and healthy fat such as chopped nuts, sunflower seeds and olive oil with or without balsamic vinegar.
Soup with lean protein, beans, and vegetables.
Sandwich with whole grain bread, lean protein, low fat mozzarella cheese, veggies, and hummus spread.

Dinner:
Lean protein such as fish or chicken, side of grilled vegetables or salad and whole grain roll with extra virgin olive oil.
Homemade pizza with whole grain pizza crust, low fat mozzarella cheese, tomato sauce, and your choice of veggie toppings (may also add lean protein such as chicken or turkey).
Soups, stews, or casseroles containing whole grain pasta, beans, low fat cheese, and vegetables.

(Many more meal suggestions and specific recipes are available online at www.synergyprograms.com, and in The SHARP Diet, available Fall, 2011)

Sample Mediterranean Snacks

Because of their lean protein and healthy fat, many Mediterranean diet foods naturally make great low-glycemic snacks – which means they keep blood sugar (glucose) levels from spiking too quickly, providing a stable energy source for the body and brain.

- Almonds
- Cashews
- Peanuts
- Mixed nuts
- Trail mix
- Whole grain bread with peanut butter
- Pita and hummus
- Low fat cheese
- 1/2 whole grain bagel and smoked salmon

Although not technically part of the Mediterranean diet, there are even some snack bars that are all natural and contain a healthy blend of nuts, fruit, and natural sugar - good choices when you need something quickly.

- *Kind* Snack Bars
- *Lara* Snack Bars
- *PowerBar* Snack Bars
- *Clif* "C" Bars
- Organic *PURE* Bars
- *Bear Naked* Trail Mix

BRAIN TRAINING for COGNITIVE FITNESS
Top 5 Exercises, and Sprint Exercises

Strength: exercises that strengthen the brain by challenging focus, attention, knowledge, speed of processing...

Top Techniques:
1. Use a training log
2. Chunk projects
3. Eliminate distractions
4. Practice mindfulness
5. Play games

SHARP Sprints:
- 5-minute laser focus
- Challenge yourself
- Move it, move it
- Count down, or up
- Red dot experience

Flexibility: exercises that enhance adaptability, positive mindset, and cultivate creativity.

Top Techniques:
1. Get Your Story Right
2. Practice Gratitude
3. Makeover Your Mindset
4. Meditate
5. Use Signature Strengths in New Ways

SHARP Sprints:
- Thank-you notes
- Visualization
- Guided imagery (sample on our website)
- Look back, and forth
- Rewrite a short story

Endurance: exercises that help sustain healthy behaviors over time, and cross training activities that give you the most return on your investment.

Top Techniques:
1. Have More Fun
2. Set SMART Goals
3. Celebrate Small Wins
4. Build Accountability
5. Do Some Good

SHARP Sprints:
- Write down your purpose
- Do an intentional act of kindness
- Add accountability
- Treat yourself
- Cross train

Cross Training –
- Laughter (positivity, relaxation, physical activity)
- Yoga (focus, positivity, physical activity)
- Meditation (focus, positivity, relaxation)
- Visualization (focus, positivity, relaxation)
- Biofeedback (focus, positivity, relaxation)

STEP SEVEN – Design and Execute Your Plan

Visit <u>www.synergyprograms.com</u> for free brain training games, guided imagery soundtrack, and more helpful tools.

Tracking tools:
SYNERGY: MyLifeGPS™ - www.synergyprograms.com - Web based tracking system to monitor progress on health & wellness behavior change.

Livestrong: www.Livestrong.com – Food and exercise logging.

MindBloom: www.mindbloom.com - A blend of technology, art, and behavioral psychology - to make self-directed personal achievement highly engaging and actionable.

Brain Training Sites:
CogniFit: www.cognifit.com - Improve cognitive health and performance for various health related conditions. Hones on the cognitive skills needed for all learning activities.

eMindful: www.emindful.com - Free 45-minute guided mindfulness meditation practice session daily. Several of the interactive classes offer CMEs for physicians and CEUs for nurses, and are taught live, by teachers who are experts in their field.

StickK: www.stickk.com - Promote a healthier lifestyle by creating "Commitment Contracts" that bind you into achieving a personal goal.

Happy-Neuron: www.happy-neuron.com/games - Improves cognitive ability through evidence-based products for individuals, cognitive therapy professionals, and employers.

Lumosity: www.lumosity.com/brain-games - Improve core cognitive skills, from attention and memory to fluid intelligence and math skills. Do better in school, perform more effectively at work, and live a more productive life.

Mayo Clinic Resilience Training: www.mayoclinic.org/resilience-training

Mind Fitness Training: www.mind-fitness-training.org - Eight-week course, specifically designed for individuals operating in extreme stress environments. MMFT provides skills training in two key areas: mindfulness skills and stress resilience skills.

MyBrainSolutions: www.mybrainsolutions.com - Matches you to exercises that are most likely to benefit you. Regularly exercising your brain in Emotion, Thinking, Feeling & Self Regulation will help you form new automatic habits that allow you to perform better in your real world activities. Interactive videos will also help you learn more about your brain, how to improve your personal brain performance, and how to improve your interactions with others.

Posit Science: www.positscience.com/braingames - Target important roots of memory & thinking.

SharpBrains: 50 Brain Teasers
www.sharpbrains.com/teasers/

Train Your Brain Meditation:
www.trainyourbrainmeditation.com

Yoga Glo: www.yogaglo.com- Online yoga classes and video streaming.

Brain Training Apps:
Brain Challenge – by Gameloft

Brain Exercises with Dr. Kawashima – by Namco Bandai Networks

Brain Toot – by Vertical Moon

Brain Trainer – by Lumosity

Brain Training Unotan – by SoftBank Selection

Brain Tuner – by Greengar – math equations

Brainwave Tuner – by imoblife - use waves patterns to relax body & mind, stimulate thought

e-Catch – by MyBrainSolutions – tuning into positive

Emotional Brain Training – by Institute for Health Solutions

ePositiveSpin – by MyBrainSolutions – optimize wellbeing with positive feelings

iJournal – by Good Think, Inc – online audio, pictures & words interactive journal

MyCalmBeat - by MyBrainSolutions – strengthen your automatic 'calm reflexes'

Split Words – by Happy-Neuron – find words assembling syllables

Apps For Remembering Names

Faces+Names – by MyBrainSolutions – their database of names, faces & job titles

iKnowYou – by PositScience – use your own names, faces & job titles

NameCatcherBiz – Catcher in the Sky – use your own names, faces & job titles

Mind Gym Workouts

The following activities provide in depth guidance for doing exercises for your brain:

Strength: Workout Your Willpower

Flexibility: Power Up Your Positivity

Endurance: Build Your Memory Muscle

Strength Training: Workout Your Willpower

Did you know that using willpower actually requires an increase in energy that creates detectable changes in your body? Anytime we have to use self-discipline to do something we aren't naturally inclined to do, our brain has to work harder. Because of this increase in activity, there is actually a shift of blood flow to the brain, as greater amounts of glucose and oxygen are needed. So why should we care?

Just like the muscles in our body, the functions of our brain need to be exercised and trained in a way that maximizes our performance. Many people assume willpower is just something we have, or we don't. But willpower, like other mental tasks, needs to be practiced. While the amount of self-discipline and willpower we have is quite limited, we can make improvements to our routine that will enable us to have the best strength possible when it comes to making healthy choices.

Willpower Training Principles

1. Train strategically – stress/recovery. Make sure not to put too much stress on yourself all at once. Any change you make is going to require some focused attention, and if it's a bad habit that you're trying to make good, it will be important to focus on a little bit at a time to avoid overloading the system (similar to overtraining in the gym). It's also critical that you give yourself adequate recovery time so that the changes you're trying to make have a chance to form more solid connections in your brain. This type of brain training allows you to take a new behavior and make it part of your "automatic pilot mode" so that it begins to be second nature and no longer demands so much time and energy.

How can you schedule your day so that you aren't putting too much strain on your energy or willpower at one time? What does your current schedule currently look like?

Monday	Tuesday	Wednesday	Thursday	Friday	Saturday	Sunday

Where could you schedule breaks during the day? Aim for at least 10 minutes off for every 90 minutes on.

Monday	Tuesday	Wednesday	Thursday	Friday	Saturday	Sunday

2. Practice – repetition builds habits. Start with small changes and begin to make them part of your routine by repeating them over and over again. This trains your brain to recognize that these changes are good, and that you need to be consistent with them. As you repeat the desired behavior, you strengthen the connections between brain cells that support this automated process. Be patient, and make sure to practice. Write it down, remind yourself, schedule it and hold yourself accountable.

What is a new habit that you'd like to create to support your management of time, energy, and willpower? Make it as specific as possible: What will you do? Where? When? How will you track it? And why is it important to you right now?

3. Create a supportive environment. One of the best ways to be supportive of yourself in making this new change is to create an environment that makes it easier for you to follow through. This means increasing the energy it takes to do the old habit and decreasing the energy it takes to do the new activity.

For example, want to watch less TV? Take the batteries out of your remote control and put them in another room. Place other options like your Kindle, a book, magazine, or newspaper close by, and you might be surprised how quickly you become OK with staying put. Want to eat more fruits and veggies? Keep cut up fruits and vegetables where they are easily accessible, in Tupperware containers or out in fruit bowls. The thought of having to make preparations is an easy deterrent, but having good choices close at hand makes them much easier to grab when you're ready for a snack.

And don't forget to add as much accountability as possible into your support system. It's much easier to talk ourselves out of something to than to try to use the same excuse to justify it with someone else. The more you talk about your commitment, the more real it becomes, and the more likely you are to create a lasting habit.

What could you do within your environment to help support you in changing this habit? Is there anything you should add or take away to make it easier? How might you decrease the activation energy required to get started?

Who will you enlist to be an accountability partner? How and when will you check in with them?

Flexibility Training: Pump Up Your Positivity

One of the most well-researched areas of brain training is optimism and positivity. A brain that is positive will perform better on nearly all functions of cognitive ability than one that is neutral or negative. As Shawn Achor describes in his book, *The Happiness Advantage*, we've been sold a bill of lies when it comes to work success and happiness. We assume that if we work hard and become successful, then we will be happy. But as studies on lottery winners and professional superstars reveal, if you're not happy before you get there and suddenly you realize that status didn't help boost your spirits, you may end up feeling even worse in the long run. The equation should read, "Be happy and work hard, and then you will be successful."

Positivity Principles and Activities

1. An attitude of gratitude. According to Martin Seligman's work at the University of Pennsylvania, one of the quickest ways to boost positivity is to think about what you're grateful for, write it down, and when possible, share it with someone else. Spending just a few seconds each morning writing down a few things you're grateful for helps you put on a lens of optimism. Our negativity bias, which is intuitive in all of us, causes us to focus more on the negatives around us in order to try to protect us from danger. But we can also get stuck in this pattern, and quickly everything around us feels like doom and gloom.

There are several ways to get a "gratitude adjustment"-
- Write down three things you're grateful for related to the day ahead.
- Write down three things you feel blessed by at the end of your day.

- Journal about things you appreciate in your life.
- Share blessing with your friends or family at mealtime.
- Write a thank-you letter to someone you appreciate.

What are you currently grateful for?

What habit could you begin training that would help you see more of the positives in your life?

Who could you write a thank you note to, and when are you going to do it (if you can't do it right now)?

2. Get Your Story Right. Many times our negativity bias is fueled by messages we tell ourselves that only make things seem worse. As Dr. Loehr states in his book The *Power of Story*, negative habits in our life inevitably come with a story that supports them.

What stories or messages might you be telling yourself that get in the way of a positive perspective? Are there any habits you're trying to change that might be stuck based on a story that is making it OK to stay right where you are?

Examples of faulty stories:
- I'll exercise later, in the afternoon sometime.
- I should eat the rest of my meal because there are children starving in other countries and I don't want to waste it.
- I feel ok, so my health must be fine.
- I'll start my diet tomorrow, so I'd better eat as much as I can now because I won't have it again for a long time.
- I would like to spend more time with my family, but they understand that I do all of this for them. I will have more time later.

What's your story? Is there a new story you could tell yourself that would move you towards your goals instead of away from them?

Remember, just because you know something should change doesn't mean it will, so telling yourself this new story regularly is a critical part of training your brain to think differently. What time of day will you commit to re-reading your new story?

3. Mindset Matters. Too many times we operate with a fixed mindset – this is how it is done because this is how it's always been done. Unfortunately, having a rigid brain limits your ability to be creative and consider other people's perspectives, and even limits your own abilities to learn, grow, and succeed.

Describe a time when you thought you knew what was going to happen but the outcome changed for the better.

Write about an experience when you were disappointed that a door closed, only to find a better one opened.

Endurance Training: Build Your Memory Muscle

Due to the constant demands on our mental energy, it's easy to feel like your memory could use a tune-up. Because we have technology to serve as our spare brains, we don't have to remember as much as we once did, which means our memory muscle has most likely started to atrophy. Remember, when it comes to our brain (and our body), if you don't use it, you will lose it!

Similar to the muscles in our body, our brain cells do not function alone but rather in groups designed to work together to complete a task. In order for us to store a memory, we have to first give it our attention, understand it, and then be able to retrieve it. Like a filing cabinet, if we do not use the right process with our storage system, the information becomes difficult to find – perhaps lost for good.

Memory 101

You have probably heard that we can only remember seven, plus or minus two, items at one time. This came from a study by researcher Miller in 1956, and while many have challenged this concept the idea seems to be fairly consistent. One change in recent memory theory is that we actually group items into chunks or units based on similarities or relationships, creating larger, more meaningful units of information. Later studies have suggested that our short-term memory capacity is more typically only three or four units of information.

There are three key "muscles" involved in our memory:

Working memory - memory as it is used to plan and carry out behavior. One relies on working memory to retain some information while working on another task – for example, baking a cake without making the mistake of adding an ingredient twice. Working memory has been said to require attention to be able to manage both short-term and long-term memory for a specific task or purpose.

Short-term memory - memory we retain for a short period of time, limited to approximately seven, plus or minus two, items of information or three to four units of related information groups (Miller, 1956).

Long-term memory – memory we retain for an indefinite amount of time, with unlimited capacity, which reduces the load on our working memory by organizing and grouping information into a smaller number of units, and encoding them into a mental filing system to be retrieved as needed.

A good mental filing system includes attention, emotion, meaning-making, narration, and repetition.

1. *Attention.* In order to start forming a memory, we need to first pay it the attention it requires. If we are constantly multitasking, it becomes difficult to commit focused attention to one thing at a time, long enough to really grasp it and begin the filing process.

2. *Emotion.* Although it is not required for a memory to be stored, when we experience some sort of emotion along with the idea or image we release brain chemicals that help solidify the connections in our mind. While negative experiences can certainly cause us to retain information, I would suggest trying to connect things with positive, funny, or even a bit risqué (this last one comes from several memory champions I researched who

said a charge of sexual energy can help memories set in concrete even more than other emotions).

3.   *Meaning making.* As part of the process of understanding, when we connect some sort of future meaning to an image or idea we make it part of a bigger picture, and therefore give it more staying power.

4.   *Narration.* Nearly all memory experts claim that the key to creating a memory with staying power is to create a story around the object you're trying to remember, and then connect the story with various images, or mental pictures.

5.   *Repetition.* Like any brain training we do, it's critical that we continue to practice so that we don't let that skill atrophy.

Memory techniques

You have probably heard of mnemonics, a memory aid that is often taught early on in school. Memory experts believe that the mind is more able to recall information that is visual, spatial, personal, surprising, humorous, or shocking. Proverbs and rhymes can also be helpful for adding staying power to information, as it makes language stand out as being unique.

In the book *A Sheep Falls Out of a Tree*, World Memory Champion Christiane Stenger talks about training strategies for improving memory. One method is a "number-rhyme" system: A rhyming word and a corresponding image are paired with each number (zero – hero, one – fun, two – glue, etc).

The more unusual the scenario you can create with the images or characters, the more likely you are to remember it. (For example, "the hero was having fun with glue." To make it stick, you decide what was fun about it based on what's fun or funny to you personally, and imagine seeing the story unfold.)

Try creating a story to memorize the following numbers: 135608

(In my story, there was a fun tree with nifty sticks that the hero ate.)

While it may be critical to win a memory competition, for most of us, remembering numbers is not a priority. But one of the most common frustrations people experience is the inability to remember names. Once again, the use of visual images and stories can be very helpful to make a name part of your permanent mental filing system.

Create images for the following names, and then create a story that brings the images to life:
Tony
Willow
Brady
Alexis
Jackie

As practice, try to pay more attention to names at your next meeting or social gathering, and use the image/story system to see how many of them you can remember.

Available Fall, 2011